Dear Pauline and Barry~

A LIGHT IN THE VILLAGE

Blessings, Light and Love on ~Your journey~

Fondly,
Hope

A LIGHT IN THE VILLAGE

*The Art of Living Life
Consciously*

HOPE WALDRON SAMUELS

Copyright © 2003 by Hope Waldron Samuels.

ISBN :   Softcover   1-4134-3174-7

Cover Photograph by Hope W. Sacharoff
Back Cover Photograph by Howard Sacharoff

All rights reserved. No part of this book may be reproduced or transmitted in any form or by any means, electronic or mechanical, including photocopying, recording, or by any information storage and retrieval system, without permission in writing from the copyright owner.

This book was printed in the United States of America.

To order additional copies of this book, contact:
Xlibris Corporation
1-888-795-4274
www.Xlibris.com
Orders@Xlibris.com
20746

CONTENTS

The Threads Of Our Beginning 11
One Day At A Time 17
Do It Anyway 21
Those He Chooses 26
Comfort Zones 32
Beyond Service 41
And Maybe Not 47
I'm Not Home Yet 52
It's The Little Things 61
Perceptions 67
Always 73
A Soft Place To Fall 78
Answered Prayers 80
Placebo Thinking 84
Window Of Possibility 90
Temptation 96
Enough Is A Feast 103
Life By Degrees 110
Pass It On 113
Feelings We Live By 119
Forty Years Too Late 125
Shadows On The Wall 129
Memories Are Better 136
The Mirror Got Old 139
Musical Chairs 143
The Need To Say Good-Bye 148
September Eleventh Two Thousand One 151

ACKNOWLEDGMENTS TO

My family of origin who did the best they could with what they had, and it was enough-
My husband, sons and daughters-in-law who continue to offer me joy, inspiration and love
all within the comfort of family-

My grandchildren's unconditional love which warms my heart and soul,
while filling any empty spaces
I may still have-
The friends of my youth, in the rooms, and those newly made who were, are still, and have become
extended family-
To those offering suggestions, while being my support group, I mention, Kaye Brown,
Faye Cherrington, Carol Fiedler, Helen Haddad,
Mike and Jeannine Venezia-

The two most memorable mentors anyone could have
<>
Yvonne and Elisabeth

And to God with whom all things are possible!

Whatever can I say in gratitude?
Until other words come along
Thank you, thank you, thank you!

Hope Waldron Samuels

ABOUT THE BOOK

Asked in 1994 how my husband and I could consider moving to a completely new area, I immediately gave what I thought was an appropriate answer. However, the answer, so quick in coming, forced me to write about it to make sure all my i's were dotted and t's crossed.

That was the beginning. With (Do It Anyway~), the Pandora's Box of my life's adventures and lessons came quickly into view. These experiences and lessons, all mine, encompass a lifetime not yet concluded . . . Welcome to "A Light in the Village."

Hope Waldron Samuels

THE THREADS OF OUR BEGINNING

The world before time,
Before we breathed air,
And saw the flight of eagles
Or heard the wings of the butterfly,
We were on a tether,
One that reached from heaven,
Connecting all that ever was
And that would be.

Whatever became of that quiet,
Ethereal place,
Infused with heavy silence,
Pregnant with possibility?
Patience? An unknown.
Everything was, nothing
To wait for.
The humming and buzzing that
Swelled within the colossal sphere,
Preceded the fallen tree in the forest.

Heavy timber then, appeared only as
Tender green shoots, softly
Covering the floor of this
Womb of speculation.
Gentle breezes, wafted about,
Depositing seeds of every variety.

And in order that they might flourish,
These zephyrs whirled circuitously,
Carrying aloft tiny saturated droplets.
Visiting a gentle mist upon
Layer and layer of vegetation . . .
Mossy green, sage and emerald,
Myriads of dewy, moisture-laden,
Liquid diamonds,
Prismatic beads of delight, a
Heavenly carpet for this threshold
Of promise.

The sun, cast a soft yellow
Glow throughout the massive
Orb, while reflecting lightly
Against featherweight filaments
Floating about.

Solitary threads
Dipping and diving,
Arching and sweeping
Endlessly through space.
With the minutiae of primal
Deva held onto each strand.
Mere specks floating in
The boundless, untouchable expanse.

Rich melodies . . . formed by
Heavenly vibrations,
Issued forth, from end to end.

Angelically sweet,
Flowing, wave upon wave.
Notes, cascading
In every range.
Perfect phrasing.
Even of the silence...
Harmonic sounds, patterns
Intricately woven,
Measure upon measure, net over net,
Fashioning the huge outer layer
Girding the universe.

Sounds emanating from the
Earth plane vibrate, even
Sounds of the Soul held
Inward, repressed, and thwarted
Are broadcast through the vapors
Of our exhalation,
Out there,
Where others can breathe in
The air of our anxiety and
Make it their own.
Or infuse the vapors of joy
To enliven their spirits,
Causing their Souls to dance.

So it was then, in the beginning...
Threads of thought, intricately woven
Into reality by a Supreme Being,
Where all was absolute.

A place for everything,
And everything in its place.
A habitation, magnificent . . .
The ultimate in glorifying
God Almighty . . .
God's House.

Was it God's ego that
Surfaced then, with the need
To be praised, for such
A spectacular dwelling?
Was His saying "and it was good" . . . not enough?
Or was it His need to share such
Magnificence with beings
Created in His own Image, the
Impetus that beckoned us forth?
Not the us, as we are
Today,
A very different creature.

One of simple nature.
Without guile.
Who bore the mark of
His Creator.
With the capacity to
Enjoy the abundance
That was all around.
With no concept of
The need for more.
There was no hunger that
Was not met with its
Appropriate balm.
Then, the fall from Grace.

When did the whispers of
Dissatisfaction and discontent
Begin to rumble?
Was it with Adam and Eve
And their curiosity?
Hers in particular?
Was it the undulating visage
Of temptation that caused her
To cross the line?
Or, just plain open
Defiance of the rules?
Actually, what does it matter?
The point is that God
Had a plan which came to pass
With the expulsion of Adam and
Eve from the Garden of Eden.
The first dysfunctional family,
Where jealousy, murder and greed ran
Rampant.
Setting into motion
The journey for us all.
The intention? . . .
No free ride.

The proviso?
Only if He were asked.
And since He held the blueprint for each
Soul, His Will would be the
Determinant in delivering
What was needed.
How fortunate for us if our wants
Coincided with His needs for us.

So from the very start
It was His Will that spun the
Wheels on which our lives
Revolved.
At first the wheels moved very
Slowly.
Perhaps in order to make sure that what
We so fervently prayed for was
Truly in our best interest.
To give us time to consider,
And reconsider.

In looking back over our lives there
Is much gratitude for the denial of
Much of what "we needed".
Whatever would we have done
Had some of those prayers been
Answered in the affirmative?

This is what we now need to look at.
How far have we come?
How well have we learned the lessons?
Do we really listen?
Are we truly co-creators with Him?
Is He pleased with our contributions?
Are we?

ONE DAY AT A TIME

As we begin to play at the
Game of life, the pieces we are given
Move on the board very slowly,
Allowing us ample time to
Think far enough ahead to
Make the right moves.

However, as the level of
Difficulty increases,
So does the speed.
Imperceptibly, the pace
Quickens.
And if we are not sure,
Not strong enough in our own convictions,
Confusion takes over,
Forcing us to rely on the opinions of others.
Ultimately resulting in decisions that
Fall short of the mark for us.
Because if there is one thing
Of which we can be certain,
It is that out there, beyond our frame
Of reference, are those very well versed
In their truth, ready and willing
To impart their philosophy, shed
Their light however diffused upon
Our path.
It is then incumbent upon us to
Find the time to make the effort,
To take that journey within.
To know ourselves.

Do we crave solitary comforts?
Does the idea of engaging
In singular pursuits
With the banner of accomplishment
Waving at our side resonate
Deep within our Souls?

Would we rather deal with
The energy of little ones
With all that that involves,
The teaching, the sharing
And the exhaustion?

Have the glances of dear friends
And family pushed us over the edge,
And in a frenzy of people-pleasing,
Thrust us among the ranks of those,
Whose lives are balanced precariously,
Between saving, and spending for themselves,
Or selflessly bearing the survival of
Another upon their shoulders?
These are easy questions
Compared to those that will
Confront us later.

Looming larger than life then, is our
Willingness to accept, that the reins
Of reasonableness and appropriateness
Have been relinquished.
Knowing the horses will
Pull in every direction,
Trampling upon the Sacred Path that
Was our own.

The challenge lies in finding our way back.
This can be done by gently retracing our
Steps in order to find the starting point
Where it all came undone,
Or spending a lifetime of hardcore investigation,
To reach the source.
Full concentration leveled at dealing
With the past, in an effort to pick up
All the dropped stitches, will
Force us to lose sight of the here
And now, because of the investment of
Time and energy focused on the other and
What little time allotted to us
Appears to speed up, to accelerate.
How futile to spend our days in such pursuit.

We are each given an investment of twenty-four hours.
Spent in joyful pursuit, doing God's Will,
Can be as rewarding as it gets.
Mired in the debris of the past,
Offers up only confusion, blinding us from right
Choices distilling the essence of our
Being.
And it does not stop there.
Because we are stalled in the investigation,
We are still confronted daily with
Choices to be made, but since the
Breeding ground has been sullied with perplexities,
The path becomes more and more muddled.
Is this what we really want for
Ourselves, or more importantly what
God wants for us?
Most assuredly not.

Our lives should be an open-faced
Sandwich, better yet, a smorgasbord
With everything laid before us,
An endless variety of delectable morsels,
Not there to tempt as in "forbidden fruit,"
But to entice.
Allowing us to make our choices
From an exciting array of opportunities.
No hidden agendas, no dark corners
Of the mind immobilizing us
To the gentle promptings that God
Would have us take, as He leads us
To His Will for us.
But how to get to that emotional
Nirvana?
It will require work, but we
Do not have to go it alone.
As a matter of fact it is not an
Ideal do-it-yourself project.
With the help of a gentle, caring Guide
Who can journey with us, help us
To face our fears head on, trace them
To their beginnings, and herein lies the key,
Alter the scenario, thus changing the end result,
Allowing us to emerge from the experience
Lighter and freer.
Remembering that "the past
Is our heritage,
The present our responsibility
And the future our challenge," *
Offers us only today, which if
Lived well, is enough, giving us ample time
To do what we must . . .
One day at a time.

---

* From a speech given by Gloria Morrison at Rosh Hashanah Services, September 17, 2001.

DO IT ANYWAY

Flashes of light
Touch every thought
As I ponder a move
That will take us
Very far away.

There are moments when
My heart soars with excitement
At the possibilities,
Followed by periods of
Quiet, feeling we are
Abandoning our children.

This is not so.
I need to remember
That both sons are married
With lives of their own,
Committed to their young families,
As it should be.

We are not content however,
My love and I to wait for
Magic moments scattered
Over time to be shared with us.
We need to take whatever time
We have left and run with it
Wherever the road may take us.

We need to wake up
To our own excitements,
The joys of our making.

It is not enough to live in the
Shadow of someone else's radiance.
The real warmth comes from living
In one's own.

This will be difficult.
Change is difficult even for the better.
Because there are always
Choices to be made.
So many sides to look at.

Our window of opportunity is not
As large as it was forty years ago.
We need to plan a new beginning
And do it now, while we are both
Able to chart the course.
We need to feel the feelings
And do it anyway.

The gentleness
Of my grandson's small hand
Touching my arm as I read
Him a story . . . the impish grin
And spirited play of his brother . . .
The flirtatious look and sweet
Smile of our beautiful granddaughter
Taking her first steps into tomorrow.
The friends whose lives have touched ours
And beyond that melded into our family
Of choice.
This is where the difficulty
Lies.

Yet, there is an upside.
New places to visit,
To explore.
Places that will rejuvenate
The spirits of young and old
Alike, adding new and fresh
Colors to the tapestries
Of our lives.
All our lives.
Expanding the horizon
Literally, allowing us all
To be part of the familiar,
While propelling us into
The unknown.

The ultimate adventure.
Our families before us
Hungered for a room with a view.
They did not have the chance.
They were caught by circumstance.
Stuck in the quagmire of co-dependency,
Disavowing their own entitlements,
To watch and wait for those
Before them to call to them
In need.
Never to enjoy the fruits of
Their labor.

We have both done well
By our children.
They are strong and kind,
With capabilities far beyond
What we could ever have imagined.
Each one has within, everything
He will ever need to make a world
That works.

There is no need for them
To look beyond themselves for
Strength and courage.
God has so blessed them.

With their wives
They are complete.
Balanced.
Each one a unit, together
A dynamic force.
All have differing viewpoints,
Yet each has strengths and weaknesses
Enough to compensate for the other.

Ultimately, a mother's function is
To fix, to make better.
This is no longer my role.
I have graduated to that of
Observer.
For me, being here
Seems as though I am waiting
For the boys to return from school.
This is not real or healthy.
That time has passed.
Today they are fathers making sure
The lessons are learned and the road
Is clear of obstacles for their children
And so it goes.

Now we need to go out
And play, resting in
The knowledge that God is
In charge and all will
Be well.
We need to demonstrate
Our confidence by giving them space.

Space to grow . . . to take chances . . .
To glory in the victories life
Has to offer.
We will visit, share letters,
Pictures, videos and use
The telephone.
They are there to tie up all
The loose ends of
Lives in transit.

No matter where we are we
Are all connected.
Through the spirit, the soul
The here and now and beyond time.
This I know.

The sun will set on the old
Neighborhood.
We will pass through familiar
Streets, and with the leave-
Taking the memories will be
Caught there for all time like
Photographs.
Each place holding a part of our lives.

With the distancing and change of view
Our pain will ease.
This kind of move will not be easy.
Nothing worthwhile ever is.
But the risk lies in not taking
The risk . . . not stretching and reaching
Beyond the experience of now.
So we will brush the tears aside
And do it any way.

The Beginning . . .

THOSE HE CHOOSES

In the world of spiritual affairs,
The concept of being a vessel,
From which the wisdom of the Universe
Is poured, is frequently talked about.
And many are chosen to play that
Role.

One question I have is,
Are those selected, aware of it when it happens?
Are they willing co-creators with Him?
Or does it happen in spite
Of themselves?

If they had a sense of their participation
In such a venture, would the immensity
Of the work cause such self-deprecation
As to invalidate the experience?
Or is being totally unaware of one's
Involvement in the scheme of things
A necessary part of the Master Plan?

I can think of instances where
Verbalizing, or writing about
Truths that are clearly
"Seen" have come about without
The bearer of such tidings having a
Clue as it related
To what was going on in
Their own lives.

It did not compute.
It did not pass go,
It did not collect anything.
The part of the brain that registers
Awareness of self was not involved.
It was short circuited from the activity.

Someone I know does channeled writing.
By placing your hand to her forehead
She is able to write the Guide-sent
Messages longhand.
It is never the same handwriting twice,
And she is not able to read it back.
Therefore she says the words, as they appear, into
A recorder, allowing the recipient of the reading
To "get the message."
Simply put, we may be selected
To deliver the message
Without it having any impact on
Our own lives.

A direct throwback
To the statement perhaps, "Do as I say,
Not as I do."

It requires a great deal of discernment
On our part to take at
Face value, the messages shared by
Those, whose lives in our
Perception, fall short of the message.
But then, who are we to judge?

Is that not the same as entertaining
And being hospitable to all, for
They may be angels unaware?
That our lessons may come in unexpected
Ways, and from those whom we would least
Imagine?

Maybe that's the plan.
A covert operation.
Acting anonymously.
Where those chosen, are people
Who ask on a daily basis for
His will to be shown, along
With prayers for the power and
Willingness to carry it out.

Or could the messages be
Delivered by example?
Where we are shown the hows
And whys by witnessing others'
Foibles and successes.
What needs to be present there,
Is the basic understanding
That life is a classroom and that
"When the student is ready the teacher
Will appear."

Perhaps then, in a greater sense
We are all teachers,
Passing along for better or worse
Answers to questions that puzzle
Us.

However I refer here to those
Who have the bigger pieces to the
Puzzle.
Who by their gifts are able
To cut to the chase, pare down
To the core, and see with such
Clarity, the seeds of truth that
Flower within life and
Death issues, they often result in
Immediate transformations.

Graduating from childish
Pursuits to that of assembling
The larger pieces of Life's Puzzle
Amid the realm of Virtual Reality,
Is a gift relegated to the few,
Those totally engaged.
Connected to that part of the Universe
Which allows them to see the intricacies
Of it all.
Scattered minutiae falling quietly
And efficiently into place.

And more than that,
Making perfect
Sense.
What most of us crave
Desperately.

There is also within each of those
Gifted souls, a very well-developed inner
Ear, whose evolution has
Furnished them the ability to
Hear God's whispers.
Their streams of consciousness run
Clear, having the muffled
Sounds of earlier visitations
Cleansed repeatedly.
Old souls.

Their vision is also exceptional.
A very active third eye is usually
Present, focusing on all manner
Of activity, with the ability to
Sift through the trivia
Of daily life, salvaging only that
Which is pure truth, leading to
The Golden Path to the heart.

Since no meeting is accidental,
Those we meet along the way help
Us to uncover things about
Ourselves, our lives, that either
Need to be passed on because
They work, or worked on because
They don't.
Back to the reason for our being
Here, simply to
Learn lessons.

That said, we are required to be
Present, open and willing.
To witness, to allow,
And to receive.
To be still long
Enough to hear His promptings, while
Catching glimpses of the Golden
Thread, tying up all the loose ends.

Learning to extricate our noses
From our navels, long enough to
Contemplate what is to be done, will
Enable us to do it, in a selfless
Focused manner, gracing the exercise
With immeasurable power.
Touching all whose lives
Touch ours.

So here's to living life
With all our senses actively
Engaged as if much depended
On it, because in reality, it does.

COMFORT ZONES

While looking for the right place
To spend the rest of our lives,
An area of infinite
Beauty and spirituality
Presented itself.

A resort community,
Offering refuge and
Pleasure.
Time out from all the craziness
The world had thrown our way.

We approached the new venture
Expectantly,
Focusing strictly
On how it would meet our needs by
Addressing our zones of comfort.
The serenity here, made the
Task of relocation less difficult.

We opened ourselves to this
Wonder-filled place
For our fresh start.
The heat of summer found us
Dividing our time at our
New destination,
Unpacking boxes,

Two hundred and fifty to be exact,
And cooling our heels
And other body parts in the
Refreshing water of the
Community pool.
One day seeped into the next.

Fall came without fanfare,
But, with a reduction of heat.
Beautiful sunny days played on.
There was no pressure for what *I*
Needed to do. I basked in the
Quiet oasis.

However, as I communed daily
With my Higher Power, concern
Over what He had in mind for
Me to *do* "out here", began to surface.
While I waited patiently

For an answer, I read books
And listened to tapes.
Suddenly, I sensed my pleas to Him
Were perhaps not properly phrased,
Impeding the response
I was looking for.

Yes, He was showing me what
To do. Set up a comfortable
Home, bathed in peace and
Light for all who enter to
Soak up the spirituality
That is all encompassing,
Along with guiding me in
Self nurturing, so long in coming.

But, what to *do* here?
What did He have in mind for *me?*
At last I found it.
In the phrase, "God, how can I be of service?"
The key.
No sooner said
Than done!
The calls came that very day.
Each different,
Both requesting service.

Excitement, coupled with humility
Was the order of the moment.
My mind could scarcely comprehend
The speed at which my request was
Answered.
I suppose,
As in all communication,
Higher Consciousness included,
Proper procedure
And clarity are vital.

I ran to meet the first
Challenge head on.
Introducing youngsters to
The rudimentary requirements of theater,
Drama, putting them in touch with
Parts of themselves most likely
To benefit from this creative endeavor.

I brought along some monologues
To whet their appetites.
Their participation was most
Gratifying.

I was told, at best, their attention
Would be fractured, and at worst
Their presence might resemble
A nomadic stream.

Such was not the case.
They all, in spite of never
Having met me before, not hearing
My message, suited up, showed up
And stayed put.

I felt the excitement
That is the teacher's lot.
The thrill of not knowing when, but
Feeling that someday, somewhere,
Something I said, would float to the surface,
Presenting the right piece to fit their puzzle,
Making a difference.
At that point in my life
Nothing else seemed quite as rewarding.

The other opportunity,
Only dressed in that garb,
Was to be a bit more obscure.
Someone, a person of letters, an
Intellect, and healer, was incapacitated,
Needing assistance in answering the
Correspondence that still poured into her
Home daily, due to the monumental
Worldwide contribution she had made.

Not being certain as to
The contribution *I* would be making
And having restricted myself to
Traveling locally, I immediately
Assumed she would be too far away

For me to have any impact.
However, as I inquired of her whereabouts,
I was asked
"Do you know your front gate?"
Then was told she lived right across the road.
Less than a mile . . . ! "Really?"
God's hand in the mix?
Both these opportunities
Came as a result of imploring
My Higher Power for direction,
Hence the proximity of this second
Recipient was most definitely
Seen by me, as Divine Guidance.

Initially, our meetings were less
Than gratifying to me.
Not that they really needed to be.
After all *I* was the one doing service.
But at the same time, I began to
Notice the anger I felt along
With the intimidation.
Each visit, left me feeling
Hurt, and reduced to
Childhood feelings of inadequacy.

My reaction
To all of this was interesting.
Thinking initially, "I don't need this
The criticism is too much for me to bear."
Yet I decided to stay, not out of
A sense of commitment, which I had, but
There was something more.
I stayed because I realized
School was still in session.

That here, in this place, right then,
Was a teacher, so exceptional in every facet
Of living, that to walk away for reasons
As juvenile, as hurt feelings, would be doing
A great disservice to myself.

What came to mind were the old fairytales.
The little girl walking alone in the
Forest coming upon a wizard who
Tells her if she can manage to
Go through all the challenges the
Forest would present, ultimately she
Would come upon a crystal goblet, so deeply cut
And exquisitely etched, that when caught
In the light of the Sun, it would
Reflect throughout the
Entire universe, its radiance
There for all to see.
Heralding her as a
Special Child of God.
A Vision Quest.

The journey began right there
In that house.
The first requirement,
Open the Pandora's Box
Of faulty messages.
The Gospel according to family.

Being totally objective, this
Sage dissected life, into
The Rube Goldberg contraption
It really is.

She is truth personified.
There is no wondering
About how she feels.
You are told.
Out loud.
In no uncertain terms.
About anything, and
Everything.
It was then, that
I imagined her small frame
Arched against the winds
Of war, with the pain
And suffering of so many
Encompassed about her,
Standing tall, on her ground,
And for all who were unable
To do so for themselves.
But that was then, and
This is now.

In truth her comfort zone
Has been violated,
By the ravages of physical impairment.
No longer able to take off
At a moment's notice, to
Whatever part of the globe
Would require her talent,
No, her genius, she is
Now dependent on others for
The simplest things.
Her meals.
Having her bath drawn, having
Her physical needs met.

Imagine someone so independent
Having to let go of her view
Of life as she knew it, while
Having to settle for another's idea of
What it should be?
For those of us desperately in need
Of being in control, it just may be
Too difficult to imagine.

And yet, we will all arrive at
That place where we have to
Relinquish control over what we
Hold most sacred to us,
How we do everything.
Won't we? Sometime?

It then becomes a matter of grace.
Doing it with grace.
Mustering all the charm you can,
Biting your tongue and accepting the
Service that others offer willingly,
If not perfectly, at least
Willingly, in spite
Of ourselves.
And not only that.
While all this is going on
Expressing gratitude.
It is the ultimate in juggling.
Keeping up one's spirit,
While your world crashes down
Around you.

Accepting other's help such as
It may be,
Graciously.
Surrendering to the inevitable
With humor.
Exhibiting more courage with
This behavior, than you
Could ever imagine possible.

And lastly, showing gratitude
For these handmaidens of God
Being a part of your life.

In the end, having accomplished this
Monumental feat, you will know
Comfort in each and every zone,
Emotional, mental, physical, and spiritual,
Resting in the awareness that in spite of
What the karmic winds have blown your way,
You have met life head on,
Totally accepting.
While miraculously hearing yourself
Say, how lucky you are!

BEYOND SERVICE

Much has been said in
Religious circles, and
By caring individuals
About the gift of service.
How mutually beneficial
For both the giver,
And receiver.
By giving, one lets go of his
Own agenda, thus opening himself up
To being there for someone else.

The recipient, basking in the comfort
Of having someone close at hand, to do
Their bidding, relieves their
Distress, concerns and anxieties,
Often getting a second lease on life.

Not much is expected in return,
If the service is pure.
Payment is extracted in feelings
Of satisfaction, at being able
To do God's work.

Though one can wish for gratitude
In the way of gentleness on the part
Of the beneficiary,
That may be too
Much to ask, given the
Circumstances facing the one
In need.

The truth of the matter as
I see it, is very simple.
What is required, of the one giving service,
Is the overwhelming desire to
Do just that.
Give service.

Having said that, there arises
The question, of how long one
Should continue the practice, when
In reality the good feelings have
Begun to deteriorate.
Veering away from
Feeling warm all over at
The joy of being there,
To major dissatisfaction.

Being bossed around in tones
Abrupt, and curt,
Receiving criticism, for things that
Skirt the boundaries of the
Relationship, call for an
Immediate review of
What is taking place now,
In spite of better times
Spent previously.

I had to see what this
Giving of myself and my time
Was ultimately costing me.

If I came away
From the encounter, muttering to
Myself, pushing down feelings
That needed to be addressed, but weren't,
For fear they would do

More harm than good,
Then I may have been acting at cross-purposes,
Doing myself a great disservice.
For instead of a warm steady glow, I
Treated myself to a slow burn.

The one in my care,
Amazingly intuitive,
Could discern quite readily
Energy that had now become
Stifled and grudging.
Certainly something to have been
Avoided if my service was to
Be selfless.

Feeling that
I had been manipulated,
Reduced the gift to something
Empty and worthless.
And so I asked myself, is that what I
Wanted my offering to be?
Certainly something much less
Than was intended when I started.

Staying then, required me to
Walk a very fine line.
Wanting to continue because
Of the concept "there but
For the Grace of God go I,"
Versus the consideration that
By continuing to overlook
What no longer worked,
I was enabling the behavior to continue,
Thus adding to my stress.

Living in close proximity
Delayed further the need for
Help to be found that would
Appropriately fill
The need.

Calls were received anytime
The mood struck,
To help with the minutia of daily living,
Which then required much soul-
Searching on my part,
Especially if the behavior repeated
Itself over and over, interrupting and
Derailing my train of thought, and
Daily agenda.

By being the "obedient servant,"
Suiting up and showing up,
I maintained the status quo,
Thwarting the search for someone to offer relief.
Or, in instances where others were found
They never passed muster.

Sadly, I had positioned myself
Between a rock and a hard place.
My usefulness was now tainted
With the sour milk of human kindness.

The one bright spot was that
I discovered who I was.
And where I had to draw the line,
After years of looking past the
Obvious.

What was required
Was something clearly stated
And unequivocal.
Such as, "I am no longer
Available.
I have to move on."

As necessary as this had
Become, that was also how hard it
Was to do, yet not to do it
Was no longer an option.

For in order to set boundaries
For myself, the other party would
Most surely feel the pain of my decision
And that certainly was never my objective.

Setting the intention to leave
This arena of service,
And actually doing it, afforded me,
After it was done, a feeling of
Being ten feet tall.
With the knowledge that in future,
Any remark thrown in my
Direction, which even hints at this
Kind of abuse will not be
Tolerated.
A gigantic lesson learned.
And one that was a lifetime
In the making.

Bemoaning the fact that it
Took so long, I realize
Doesn't matter
What does matter is that it happened
At all.

So now that this block of time
Is part of my history,
I can be comforted in knowing
The service I performed was
Done well, done to the best
Of my ability, and that yes,
I received payment after all.

Taking me to another
Level of awareness, where
I became engaged in the care
Of myself, knowing that when that
Comes first, I can then give
Others that which is above and
Beyond service.

AND MAYBE NOT

It has been said that ninety percent of
What we worry about never comes to
Pass.
I believe it.
As we prepared for the move that would take
Us from the world as we knew it,
We found a thorn in the flower
Of possibility.
A nagging concern that over time
Would color our perspective
Of the adventure.

Would being far from our grandchildren
Cause disavowal of us?
Would not seeing them for long
Periods of time, cause
The mental tapes of us, stored in their
Young minds to unravel
Or worse yet, fade completely?

It would seem reasonable to believe
That relationships, in order to grow,
Require regular deposits
Of quality time.

Minutes, hours, days, months
And years of one on one,
Replete with ample amounts
Of personal attention,
Love, and nurturing, all geared to
Support who they are
Becoming.
Well, maybe not.

Many manage to have
Lives, at once self-
Fulfilling and complete, while
Encompassing generational
Closeness.
Maybe the exception to the rule?

If on the other hand one is
Called to live a life of
Separation, required to do
Service apart from those whose
Lives we wish to imprint with
A part of ourselves, there actually
May be nothing to worry about.

For what I speak of here
Is the bonding, that can occur
At the time of conception,
During the swirl of post-
Seminal alchemy.
Features and tendencies which
Are passed on, without any input
Of our own.

Partial reflections of ourselves
Sometimes in a physical sense,
Or proclivities that
Spill over, reminding us
Of ourselves in a very profound way.
Abilities and leanings
Passed on in spite of ourselves.

Little ones who resonate to similar
Promptings, whose inner light is
Awakened by the same creative endeavors.
Unbeknownst to each other at the time,
Yet often recognized by family members
With strong ancestral roots.

There are those of us who have no
Visible frame of reference to draw upon.
The role model we most exemplify,
Has left the arena of day to day
Interaction, years before
We were a blip on the screen.
But who, for unexplained reasons has
Left their stamp, a genetic imprint,
To be read at a later date,
Leaving no room for doubt, as to whose
Progeny we are.

How reassuring is that?

For me, very.

The idea that this latest generation,
May have had bestowed upon them
Bits and pieces of myself
That will be given other opportunities
To accomplish what in my own life-
Time I could not, is a very hopeful sign.

I am not referring to any of this in
The ego sense.
But rather those ideas and positives
Instilled within us, now
Taking root in another, with
An eye to their fruition.
Remembering that no door is
Ever shut, without God opening
A window.

We can look on it as passing
The torch, carrying on where
We left off, or seeing the validity
Of our agenda.
Standing back, we can then relish the
Fervor they take in reweaving all the loose
Threads, with an eye to tightening
The tapestry.

It will no longer be our tapestry
To be sure,
For each is one of a kind,
But what it will be, is a design
Uniquely theirs, with colors
And patterns vaguely familiar.

That has the look of family.
Similarities that speak of blood-
Lines, talent and creative whisperings
Overlapped in a way, while taking off
In their own direction.

This is a very good thing.
Because it burrows beneath the surface,
And deals with teachers of the Spirit, the
Coaches of the Soul, where the seeds of
Posterity are planted,
And all we need do is recognize them
As such, honor them, and joyfully
Bring them full circle.
For they are a special endowment fostered
By Divine Intervention,
All out of our control
Yet fashioned in part
Out of our cloth . . .

I'M NOT HOME YET

I stand alone, in the dazzling blue
All-enveloping sky,
Surrounded by the sweet vapid smiles
Of strangers.
On endless roads with no destination.

Not long ago I was a working woman,
Rising early, selecting what I would wear,
To be with people with whom I had many
Years of vested time,
Sharing tidbits of lives
Unique, yet similar.

The mirror of our days, reflected
Our concerns about clothes, hair color,
Home and oh yes, recipes . . .
No longer for families now, but for two
If we were lucky.

Gone, the need for buying toys,
Back to school clothes, obsessing
About our children's behavior
The pattern in the Grand Design
In transition.

The busyness of my days kept me
From dwelling on the loss of my
Children to the most natural of
Things.
Adulthood.

If child-rearing is successful,
They become responsible, taking
Care of themselves without
Benefit of parent.
I went from center to far out
Overnight.
Ready or not there they go.

Regaining one's balance
After such a major shift
Took time.
It was not an event.
It was a process,
Done slowly, with
Many distractions of self
Along the way.
With the realization that in all the
Years of doing for others,
I had lost track of what it was
I needed to do for myself.

Ministrations to me, that
Had once seemed unnecessary,
Now took on major importance.
Others' preoccupation with self
Always triggered my critical voice.
Carping about their behavior
Being inappropriate, and how much
More superior my selflessness was.
Not so.
There is room for caring and
Nurturing at every level of
The human experience.
Today I know that unless I love
Myself enough to give me what I
Need, unconditional love of
Others will be hard to come by.

In looking for my true identity,
Blessed holes appeared in the armor
I had fashioned for myself.
Directives given me as a child,
Those sacred rules to live by,
Evaporated as a mist
In the light of day.

Having outgrown the clothes
Of that time, so too
The messages no longer fit.
With an awareness I'd never
Known, I took the first
Steps in finding my lost
Child.

When young, I played hide
And seek.
I was a base sticker, they said.
Afraid to leave the safety of the tree
Where I hid my eyes.
Looking from there, not
Daring to venture beyond
My comfort zone.
This was how I dealt with
Much of my life.

I chanced upon the road
On which I find myself today,
Almost nine years ago.
With the arrival of two wonderful
Daughters-in-law, I became
Aware of feelings and attitudes,
Not only inappropriate, but
Painful.
What was wrong?

In the quest I discovered
Someone I didn't like.
Who apologized profusely for
Being.
Who heard others' opinions
And ideas as criticism,
Refusing to discuss anything
Unless certain that all would be in
Agreement.
Responsibility for self?
A totally foreign concept.
He, she, they made me feel
However it was.
Sense of entitlements?
Never having heard the word before, why
Wouldn't I be content living
My life with a "less than" attitude?

Prejudging others' insides
By their outsides, was my
Knee-jerk response when
Making new acquaintances.
Incapable of saying three
Important words, "I don't know,"
Found me making up believable
Answers, instead of admitting
I had none.
Tolerate toxic relationships?
Sometimes.
Because I was into numbers.
And more was better.
Then gradually, with
Some pain and some joy,
I had an increased sense
Of what was right for me.

No longer feeling on the
Outside looking in
The work on myself finally
Paying off.

Then the word choice reared
Its' ugly head, placing me
Between a rock and a hard place.
The time had come to exercise
Its' true meaning.
A decision to make,
Allowing Providence to step in
Becoming the facilitator.

The path leading to our house
Was not visible by pillars of
Fire at night, nor clouds by day, but
Instead by the tiniest specks of light.
Pinpoints of possibility.
Just maybe we could walk into
The new adventure, totally wrapped
In sunlight.
Not wanting the leave to
Be horizontal,
Shrouded in the veil of
Darkness.
Choices, something I
Make, or not, but
Then, that too is a choice.

Time for the child
To go out and play.
Letting go and letting
God.

Ultimately He took me
By the hand and bade me
Follow.
In doing so I accepted
His invitation to Life
Part Two . . .

I offer thanks to Him
For endless days of
Spring.
Warm gauzy days, fresh with
The breath of childhood.
Cool marble floors
Beneath my feet,
With time enough to sit and
Dream in rooms where every window
Frames God's finest work.
No pressure.

The soft life.
Meaning?
Absence of harshness.
Soft edges everywhere.
People, places and things.
The face younger now, smoother.
The critical self receding,
Becoming more loving, gentle.
Yet with all the beauty, for
Eye, heart and soul,
There is an empty space
In the chain of perfection.
The desire to share it with
Those whose blood is mine.

Whose early years were spent
At the well of family life,
Where drinking from the
Same cup, gave nourishment
From the shared experience.
That part of me which cries out
For them to see and feel
About it as I do.

Yet, I know this cannot be.
What I bring to this new life
Is just that, my offering.
No longer a familial effort.
Where before, in the democracy
Of the household, we would take a vote,
I now win by a landslide.
Knowing that the move took place
Because somewhere deep inside
A chord was struck,
Erasing the need to hold
On to all that had been played out.

The quiet that I always longed
For is here.
The beauty of land and sky
Is all around me.
The sense of loss?
Some.
But more than that, it's learning
To deal with the unfamiliar.
In time, this will all be
Comfortable.
We do delight in the company of
New friends,
Those too, who decided to
Come out and play.

It has been said "be
Careful what you ask for,
You might get it."
I am grateful arriving
At that place, where
My wants coincide with
What God has in mind for me.

This has become a world
That works, only because my
Will and my life are turned
Over to the God of my
Understanding, every day,
One day at a time.
I no longer have my
Hands in the "mix"
Manipulating the ingredients . . .
Forcing the outcome.

The sense of separation . . .
Distancing myself from all
That was familiar,
Will evaporate, when
Those so dear step across
Our threshold.
Their energy, together
With the spark of
Recognizing like selves
Will infuse the space with
Joy.
The joy of rediscovery.
I believe it will be at that moment
The house will metamorphose
Becoming what we had envisioned
All along, our new home.

Those sweet voices will enter
The fiber of my being,
Spreading out from me in all
Directions, touching every
Timber, becoming part of the
Ether.
Resonating in these
Rooms forever.
But until then,
I'm not home yet.

IT'S THE LITTLE THINGS

Wherever I am today,
For me to see how
Far I've come I need to
Look back.
The distance is whatever my
Mind says it is, "just like
Yesterday," or "a hundred
Years ago." The proximity
Solely dependent, I believe,
On the issues most needing work.

The child within
Has waited a lifetime
To be recognized, let
Alone cared for.
So, while inching along slowly,
Looking for ways to nurture, protect
And honor myself,
Maturity, hovers in the
Wings doing push-ups.
Preparing to thrust itself
With all its power, if not glory,
Literally in my face.
(Testifying to that requires
Only that I look in the mirror,)
Where finding my child
Amongst the furrows and myriad lines
Of experience, becomes
Harder and harder to do.

Having days of serenity and focus,
To investigate the needs
Of my child,
With little else to concentrate on,
Should enable me to search out the
Delicate flower of my soul,
Offering it the elixir best suited
For its growth.

But, the glimpses that I *am* afforded
Are not that smooth, uncluttered,
Nor focused.
Instead what comes into view
Are core issues dealing with
My reactions to others' behavior
Either directed at me, or someone else.
I never noticed, if they
Were totally my perceptions,
As they related to my story,
Knee-jerk responses if you will,
Or if they were strictly
Others' behaving badly, and
My reacting appropriately.

Sour attitudes toward
Another can have its
Roots nestled in the cradle.
Almost like one's agenda
Coming in.
Men who speak to their wives,
Disrespectfully, the wife stating that
"He spoke to his mother the same way,"
Or "Oh well he's always been like that."
Triggers the old saw that
"Two wrongs don't make a right."
And they don't, ever.

There is for the one who
Is the receptor of these verbal
Attacks, a large price
To pay for simply being quiet.

Each, and every word,
Makes a mark upon the soul
That after time, forms a
Lesion, ugly and hard.
The center of which,
Remains soft and oozes the
Life Force slowly, while
Opening itself up to
Dis-ease.

Is it any wonder then,
Upon closer examination, that
So many souls are
Burdened with life-threatening
Situations, which might
Never have occurred?
Ever—
Had there been an awareness of
Their connection to
A Power greater than themselves.
Knowing, that as beloved
Children of God, they were furnished,
As their birthright, a protective
Shield, to keep at bay
That which would
Damage His creation.

Often in such cases the karma exacted
Against those who perpetrate these
Infringements, does not
Come swiftly enough.

While usually the one who bears the brunt
Of the assault, leaves the
Earth long before,
Adding confusion, as to the
Lesson to be learned here.

The work then, as I see it is to reach
The Higher Self, where
One speaks up, no longer giving
Anyone the right to demoralize,
Denigrate, or desensitize any-
One so completely, that they lose
Sight of their rightful inheritance.

I have now said that twice.
That we are given a
Protective shield as our birthright,
Unconditionally, so to speak,
With one proviso,
That we ask God for it
Daily.
And that may be the rub.

For we need to sense
That some harm is in the offing,
That what is being presented is not
Acceptable behavior.

It is my feeling that
Another opportunity to re-inhabit
The planet, will be given to all.
Those whose lives are brief,
Peppered with discomfort,
As well as to those who dispense the pain,
Along with the opportunity to make
Very different choices the next time.

The question is, how many times
Has it been, this next time?
And, if as they say, an
Angel appears to us at
Our birth
Sweeping from our minds
Everything that has occurred
In the life before, what
Are our chances for different
Responses?
How do we recognize when
Something that we sense as familiar,
May refer to something from
Another time and place?

The same, as visiting
A place for the first time,
Sensing somehow that
We have been there before.
It's the little things.
A fragrance, a sound, a visual,
Lasting perhaps only
A second, bringing to
Mind a whole scenario
Of prior events.

So it can be then with pain.
Somewhere deep inside ourselves
It registers as an old wound.
Familiar.
Triggering a prior image.

Being quiet and going into that
Place, that former residence where
Our soul bore witness to exploits
That rendered us incapable of

Survival, causing us to shut down
Leaving us totally incapacitated, while
Hearing in the soul, faint whispers
Of recognition.
It is then on that level that
We begin to see the source.
Bypassing the "rote response."

We will not bleed to death
By biting our tongue, nor
Will taking a breath in
Order to be assured that our
Perceptions are correct,
Lessen the impact we will have.
Because knee-jerk responses are not
Called for here.
And by doing the former we
Prevent further karmic damage.

Yes, it is the little things,
Closing the eyes,
Breathing deeply,
Searching for that former
Reference point.
But most importantly,
Paying homage to that shield
Of protection, pulling it
Close around us, while
Giving thanks for its presence.

Not really a little thing at all.

PERCEPTIONS

As I see it
What passes for
Family life today, is not recognizable.
What was important when I was
Creating a close-knit family,
Seems to have deteriorated, fallen away.

Was my creation made entirely out of
Whole cloth?
Loving and appealing on the outside,
Unhealthy and dysfunctional beneath the surface?
Is that what I fashioned?
I would hope not.

Parents now, profess
Mostly by their actions,
That discipline, respect, and caring behavior
No longer define
Quality of life.
What does, is open to conjecture.

I understand each generation feels they
Have all the answers,
Their private pact with destiny,
Swearing upon the heads of their children
Never to repeat the mistakes
Visited upon them.

Honorable, if not somewhat idealistic.
To fashion something
Distinctly their own, but how?
By dropping the stitches
Off the needle that gave integrity
To the garment?

Ultimately, even with the purest
Of intentions, the wall of
Generational recidivism surfaces
Blocking their view.
Reminiscent of looking into a
Mirror, looking into a mirror,
Looking into a mirror, images
Superimposing one upon the other,
Receding further than the eye can
Fathom.
Driving one mad in the attempt.
Ideally, a vision,
Capturing the colors of today, while
Incorporating those of times past,
Would add richness and dimension to the cloth,
As well as strength.

Generational differences,
Perception,
Role models at different stages of development,
All play their part in fashioning the
Intricate, unique design
We call life. Most particularly
Our life.

So much of what we see
In family, partners, and
Co-travelers, is a reflection
Of ourselves that either delights us
Or begs improvement.

Whether living in the light,
Or in the shadow of others,
Each of us at the table of life's
Experience walks away with
Entirely different perceptions of
The meal.

Some, well-nourished, satisfied with less,
Pass through life, anxious to give service.
Others embittered by the encounter,
Walk away from the meal, and sometimes
From the table altogether, unable to give
Even to themselves.
Abandonment of self, contributes to the
Starvation of the soul, that tender, most
Vulnerable part, which commences to wither
And harden, causing the spirit's flame
To falter, wavering between eruption
And extinction.
An existence at risk,
All due to self-denial.
To be with someone whose intellect is intact,
Who can articulate the proper behavior
For any given circumstance, but who on
The Spiritual and emotional level, is totally
Unable, or more precisely unwilling to
Walk the walk, is painful to witness.
Anger at God for meting out difficulties
That require hard work, offer distorted
Perceptions of what it's all about.
Put simply, life is a classroom.
No more, no less.
We need to sort through the inexhaustible
Debris that washes up on our shores in order
To get through to the other side.

That side where clarity and satisfaction
Of a lesson well learned usher in warm
Feelings of gratitude and pride
Of self.
Built one upon the other, day after day,
Those zones of comfort replace the
Arid arena of antipathy.
Slowly the warmth of the sun enters the soul.
Permission given, by the hard work, and
The lesson mastered.
We then concede to our entitlements,
Old behavior not allowing the reward
Before the accomplishment.

But more than that,
We acknowledge and lay claim
To all that is good.
We trust the process.
Knowing that our inner child
Is getting the balm of self-approval,
And love, buried for so long.
Suddenly as if overnight, our countenance
Takes on a radiance, matched only by the
Lightness of our step.
We have deposited the
Baggage of guilt, resentment and misunderstanding
At the feet of our Higher Power, intoning
The words, "Thy will, not mine be done..."
And "God is in charge, all my needs will be met."

We are then faced with a truth,
The road we have traveled,
Will be traveled by all.
At one point or other, each of us, will be
Faced with decisions that position us
Between a rock and a hard place.

How we maneuver, the twists and turns that
Propel us on our journey,
Will be God's message to us. Lessons, lessons, lessons.
Whether we choose to see it that way,
Of course, is the difference between succeeding
In the quest for inner growth or merely
Conducting the search.

We can rail against the injustices we feel
Search us out, our eyes focused everywhere but
On ourselves, and our responsibility.
Or we can recognize our Karma.
Having visited upon us, that which we have given.
And from that point, move on.

The metamorphosis will be complete
With the realization that every generation
Does its best to improve upon the preceding one.
There is no blame.
How can one fault, not wanting to stay in the
Status quo?
Until tried every concept, is just that.
An idea, whose time may or may not
Have come.

So here's to Honesty,
Faith, Courage and Patience
All necessary ingredients
In the mix of life.
And perhaps to the most important one
Of all.
Trust.

Which like a warm blanket,
Covers that part of ourselves
Shivering in uncertainty,
Hiding in the dark, so desperately
Needing to find direction.
May the warmth, it offers coax us
Into surrendering our
Innermost needs and desires
To that core place within,
Trusting that with Him all things
Are possible . . . !

ALWAYS

The darkness, is so pervasive that
Even the brightest rays of the Sun,
Offers not a fragment of light.

The place within, where nothing
Outside touches the sacred halls
Of imagined, or real experience.
Vaulted . . . encapsulated . . . locked in responses
To situations real or not,
Triggered by some thing or
Worse yet, nothing at all.

Pleas to my Higher Power, or Self,
Seem for the most part to fall on
Deaf ears.
For without the facility or
Acumen to know what to ask for, I
Am reduced to 'God please help me'
Further placing me on hold.
For someone like myself, where
Nothing can happen fast enough,
Waiting only intensifies the
View . . . inexorably dim.
The blackness, becoming
Even more impenetrable.

Looking desperately, in the past
For answers, as to what
Plagues me today, is at best
Tiring, and at worst futile.

My soul's candle offers
Only the barest pinpoints of light,
Giving up little in the way of
Solutions.
The wait is almost too much
To bear. I reach for the concept
Of living in the question.
Not to be concerned about the whys and wherefores.
Just put one foot in front of the other,
Trusting that He will provide.
The word that best describes the feeling
Is excruciating.

What is sought at its
Deepest level is Faith.
There are times when it's so simple
To give lip service to Trust and Faith.
It rolls off the tongue easily,
"I trust that . . . I have faith that . . . "
All surface communication.
Not hearing at the deepest level
What it is that I am saying.

The road on which I travel,
Tenders peace and comfort
If I can but remember that.
Offering blessed relief from the agonies that
Have plagued my mind.
The road called
Living in the moment.
Certainly not a new concept in the

World of yoga, gurus, and those
Who are
Enlightened.
However, it is not
An overnight discipline.
For myself, whose patience is
At best limited, it is
Difficult to access.

My choices are few.
Believing is not the answer either . . .
But if I can recall a time,
When something so exceptional
Occurred, something that defied explanation,
Leaving me speechless and in awe,
Introducing the realization,
Without any doubt of
God's presence,
I can then come from a place of *knowing*.
Knowing that in every living, breathing moment of
My life, God is present.
He is not a now and then concept,
Nurturing His children on a whim.
Now you see Him now you don't.
His blessings are there for me
Always.

It is not His style to
Be there randomly.
The planets do not rotate randomly.
Trees do not bud, bloom and shed their
Leaves randomly.
The seas do not ebb and flow randomly.

Nothing in the Universe
Is a random process.
It is a well thought-out plan
Accompanied with guidance every
Step of the way.
If we accept the guidance.

It sounds so simple.
A yes, or a no.
What would we give
To lessen the struggle?
We are here to learn the lessons
Most assuredly, that will point the way.
But, and this is core,
To do so with God as
Our Helper and Guide.

His will, being ours always,
Freeing us to be.
To do His bidding.
Not just now and then,
Always.
Not randomly selected, when we
Are stretched beyond self, our
Inner resources drained to the limit.
Always.
Never losing sight of the fact
That everything that occurs
Is for a reason, not randomly
Selected for *us*, but planned for us,
Always.

Then the sliver of light becomes
A beam directed at us, illuminating
Our lives, enabling us to see, if only
For a nanosecond, the emerging pattern
That is wholly *our* design.

By having the veil lifted ever so slightly,
For even that briefest moment,
We can see when we are "cause",
The way we choose to think about
Any given concern or task,
How we actively select our responses.
Then finally, with bent knees and bowed head,
With the realization,
That if not turned over to
God, while asking for
His will in the matter,
We are doomed to repeat
Those lessons, different scenarios,
Again and again.

Or, to abandon ourselves,
Taking leave of God.
For when God is not there for us, who moved?
Thus choosing to be slightly scattered.
To wander aimlessly.

The beacon of light enters
My soul, with its radiance
Spilling out from
All sides, melting the
Darkness.
Ushering in
Hope, Healing, Joy and Light.
Willingness is the key.
It must be there,
Always.

A SOFT PLACE TO FALL

When things go awry as they so
      Often do,
And my mind is scattered and such,
I may wander about, sometimes in,
      Sometimes out, with
No sightings, no whispers, no crutch.

The reasons are just about endless
      you know,
They're as varied as the planet
      itself,
The wills and the won'ts the do's
      and the don'ts,
Right now, or the eighth or the
      Twelfth.

I may then reach out to my friends,
To tap into their spin as they see it,
For their sage advice, given once
Sometimes twice, with my attitude saying
      So be it!

But then there are times
      Thank the Lord,
When weariness bends head
      and knee
And I reach up and cry
And I ask why oh, why?
And here is what He gives to
      me . . .

A voice that is tempered and
    calm
Framed in music and light just
    for starters,
The fog? It's dispelled.
My hands? They are held.
As we journey through very
    rough waters.

The search then is over for me.
For whether I stand or I fall
My surrender's complete I'll
Be back on my feet,
And that's where it's at after all.

This process can take what it takes
The time frame is not ours to judge,
To let go and let God, not a wink
Not a nod, with nary a push or a nudge.

So there's surely a place for
    us all,
To be calm and not stutter or stall
To drop all our fears
That we've gathered for years,
It's at my Father's House
The ultimate . . . penultimate
Soft place to fall . . .

ANSWERED PRAYERS

One of the first things
We learn as children
Are bedtime prayers.
Simply put and direct,
They ask God to watch over
Us as we sleep, as we suspend
Our hold on Life for
Those few hours,
Along with requesting Him
To do the same for our
Nearest and dearest.
So engaging especially from
Children newly arrived,
Fresh from their Father's house,
Replete with the balm of
Innocence.

This practice of simple
Daily contact may go on
For years and years,
Child-like in its approach.
Big on supplication, short
On tangibility.

As life becomes more complicated
And we see that left to
Our own devices, we are unable to
Manifest that which we feel we are
Entitled, our prayers suddenly
Take on a very different tone.

It is then that the
Entreaties begin.
The knees hitting the floor
In a way that speaks of desperation,
With prayers that border
On hysteria.

At this time we often
Omit the need for God's
Will to be shown, only that
He answer our prayers quickly,
And in our favor.

The requests run the gamut
Of every conceivable
Blessing known to Man.
The pleas may be tearful,
Or laced with anger.
Justified, in the eye of the
Beholder, or totally out of
Left field.

However, when the plea mirrors
His will for us, and it is in
His time,
There is nothing that can get in
The way of it happening, nothing
This side of Heaven and
Earth that will keep it from coming
To pass, except perhaps
We ourselves.

There is also another side
Of this need of ours, that I
Think has been generally
Overlooked.
The duplication of prayer.
Someone, somewhere else,
Lifting up their voice in
Need, with the same exact
Desire.
For someone to come into their
Life, in order to provide the
Missing pieces to their puzzle.

Of course we all operate under
The assumption that we are
Unique, and that no two people
Would request similar treasures.
That *we* might just be the answer
To someone else's prayers may be
A totally foreign concept.
And one that we might find
Hard to accept.
Truth be told, my guess is that
We never even entertain that
Synchronistic thought, being as caught
Up in our own needs as we are.

But sometimes we are
Faced with Divine Intervention.
That gentle nudge that beckons us to lift
Our noses out of our navel, look around
And see the Master Planner at His best.
Full of humor, bestowing the
Gift of loving kindness, with
The desire to be beneficent to
His children.

Recognizing the Master of the Universe,
As the ultimate in Minutia Management,
We also know then of His abilities
In dispensing His largesse.

The best part of the scenario however, is
When the receivers of this combined
Bounty are caught totally off guard.

It truly speaks of the Divine Hand
In a situation that would never have
Happened any other way.
It is the veil lifting ever so slightly
Affording us glimpses of what the
Concept of letting go, and
Letting God is all about.
Knowing that we are not meant to
Struggle.
That no amount of
Pushing, pulling, tugging
Twisting, with manipulations no
Matter how determined, has the
Chance of bringing forth any
Situation, if
Not meant to be.

That is why, if we live our lives
In hopeful anticipation,
Expecting miracles,
And not quitting before
They occur, we can look forward
To a life of constant joy and wonder.
Especially when the gift is twofold,
The answer to a prayer,
Twice blest.

PLACEBO THINKING

Is it ever
Appropriate
To receive, and decline
An invitation, or a calling, allowing
The overture to be enough?

Was life ever enjoyed by
Denying its offerings?
Surely not,
Not at its fullest and
Deepest level.

Isolating,
Closing down in the area
Of the shared experience,
How can that feel good?

And when that attitude
Superimposes itself upon
Reality,
And we hear ourselves say
How much better *it* tastes, well,
Just maybe, we've lost sight of
The true nature of things.

We have much to bring to
The party,
Contributions uniquely ours.
While often unaware
Of their exact nature, we
Are hard pressed to know to
What extent they will be missed.
Do we then not cheat at the
Game?
Defrauding ourselves of
Our rightful place among our
Peers,
While depriving others of
Our full potential.
Losses all the way around.
"Being nominated is enough . . . "
Is it really?
Weren't we in it
For all the marbles?
Is it not better for
Us to say "Wow! what
A disappointment," bless
The winner, and vow that
We'll be back?

By our birth
We are entitled to much,
The whole enchilada.
Not just crumbs or
Possibilities but
Realizations.
Real-life manifestations
Tangible, palpable
Not ersatz,
The real deal.

At first it may seem so
Much easier to back away
From opportunities, to
Denigrate our talent,
Dismiss with cavalier grace
The specialties with which
We are blessed.
What we may fail to see
In this seemingly selfless exercise
Is the specter of
Reverse grandiosity
Hiding in the shadows.
Oh yes, it is definitely
There.

Accompanied by slaps on the back
And pleas by those who are in
Our court to see how very
Smart, clever, witty,
Attractive or creative we
Really are, and how by continually
Feigning disagreement we fall
Into the trap of reverse grandiosity.
Extracting from others that which we
So desperately need
To bolster our otherwise
Crumbling facade.

Also, this behavior feeds
On itself continuously . . .
One dose of such fawning
Admiration begets another
And another . . . and with so
Little effort on our part.

By talking the good talk
Without taking the
Steps necessary to accomplish
The task, we literally
Live on borrowed time.

The accolades will
Fade, as does a rainbow, whose colors
Once so sharp and vivid now
Are difficult to discern.

Instead of sealing off the
Memories of the past with a steel
Door we revisit them
Continually, by dredging up
Those compliments as if
They were the latest styles.
Failing to see how outdated and
Threadbare they have
Become.

Building our lives on
Dreams and possibilities
Lacks real energy and
Because the door to the
Future is sealed as well,
What will taste truly authentic
And fortify the soul
Is being here now and doing real
Work in spite of the outcome.
Go for it.
Afraid?
Swallow it.
Let God go first and follow His
Lead.
With giant steps ask yourself
"May I?"
Then give yourself permission.
Taste the flavor of success in the
Act of making the effort.
You can deal with the results later.
Actually the results are not up
To you.

But whatever they are, you can learn
The lesson while continuing to make the
Effort.
That's Life, the real deal . . .
No longer playing
Among the shifting veils of
Pretense,
What if,

Maybe,
Thanks but no thanks.
But, instead here I am,
I will definitely be there,
Here is what I've done and
Hang the deed out there
For all to see.
Your banner of accomplishment.

You will know then, what
Real-life success is all about.
The sweet Truth of
Who you are.
Not a manufactured
Sugary confection that melts in
Your mouth, but solid, nourishing,
Sustenance, that nurtures and
Introduces
Real effort,
Real commitment,
And real results into your life's equation.
One-half of something is so much
Better than one hundred percent
Placebo!

WINDOW OF POSSIBILITY

It has been said, that "regardless of circumstance,
Each man lives in a world of his own making."
If true, why bother blaming others,
Particularly our families of origin, for where
We are today?

Could it be the word *responsibility*
Was not explained sufficiently to us
As children, keeping us
From seeing how our actions
Shape our condition?

Role models play an important part in
How we view the world.
Through the eyes of those who are
The guardians of our childhood,
We establish the frame
On which the cycle of our days is spun.

As fresh-eyed innocents, no thought is given
To the quality of information imparted to us
As gospel.
Be it right, wrong, or more to the point
Appropriate.
We are shaped and molded by remarks
And statements sometimes casual,
Often misguided, and occasionally
Cruel.
Guilt usually accompanies us on this
Early journey, with low self-esteem
Not far behind.

Much of our lives thereafter is
Spent aimlessly repeating these
Inappropriate remarks, if not
Aloud to others, at least to
Ourselves in our heart of hearts.
The worst-case scenario has us
Passing on the same faulty messages
To our offspring.

There is no solace in lashing out
At our ancestors, nor gain in
Squandering precious time
Struggling in the web of their
Negativity, yet we do so.

But wait!
Is there another way to
Look at the question of responsibility?

The search takes us to
A level of awareness, that to the
Enlightened, is familiar
Territory.
To know that nothing
Happens by accident... enables us to see
The true meaning behind
The student being ready and the teacher
Appearing.

We move on to the realization
That our sojourn on this planet
Is merely to learn the lessons
We missed the last time around,
Casting a very different light
On our situation.

One step further... and we are told to consider
That as Spirits, we select
The families in which to be born.
And that under God's direction,
They are commanded to teach *us*
What it is we need to know.

How dare we then, allow our egos
The grandiosity to criticize, or offer
Forgiveness to those, whose sole responsibility
Was to dispense the very lessons necessary to
Elevate us to another level of consciousness?

God's plan?
Fulfilling their responsibility?
Really!
A karmic maneuver,
Way beyond our control.
But then how much of life do
We control anyway?

Advancing precariously,
We navigate the rough waters of
Discovery, seeing clearly, if
We are open, those areas in our lives that are
Not working, no matter the purity of
Our intention.

What to do?
We are suddenly reduced to children,
Tired of the game,
Caught in yarn that is
Knotted and frayed, disheartened by
Puzzle parts that don't fit, by pieces
Broken or missing.

Thus begins our fall from Grace.
In the descent we quietly acknowledge our faults.
If the fall is gentle, we have time to see
The mountains yet to climb,
The lines we must not cross,
All the untapped potential.
If on the other hand we suffer a
Speedy decline, it all flashes
Before our eyes too quickly
To be specific.
Suffice it to say
That our lives have definitely become
Unmanageable.
In quiet desperation
We finally, let go.
Not always a decision
Made clear-mindedly.
Often our hands reach
Up imploringly,
As our knees, hit the
Floor in utter
Humility.
Surrender, complete and unequivocal.

Now, here's a fresh place to start.
Upon a road that we have never
Walked before, or if we have,
One touched upon so lightly,
That scarcely was a footprint
Made visible.

Some of us, afflicted with
What I call selective amnesia,
When, in an uncomfortable place,
Can never remember being elsewhere.

Conversely, while flying in air so
Rarefied, the recollection of darker
Canyons, is truly far removed.

Our eyes, now open
See for the first time
That we are not alone and
What is more, we never
Have been.

It was necessary for us to hit bottom to
Admit that our certainty about everyone
And everything was often flawed.
That running through life, does
Not require a hammer and tong,
Or for that matter a machete.

That we can, given our new insight
Be the parent of that beloved child of God
Within ourselves, whose behavior all these
Years, has been a clarion call,
Not for correction and criticism,
But rather, for nurturing, warmth
And unconditional love.
Commodities all too rare
But nonetheless precious.

We talk today about a level playing field,
But those of us conscious of where we've been
And where we're headed,
Find it more a spiral, spinning us through
Time and space, taking us to levels
We never thought possible,
With vistas far beyond our wildest dreams.

Such a climb is a heady experience to be sure.
One that requires a light touch
Removing from our shoulders the burdens
Of the past, setting aside the seriousness
Of the effort, while looking at each adventure
As a lesson offered.
Putting an entirely different spin on the
Journey.

We are works in progress,
By no means a done deal,
With a willingness which is key
To sort through the flotsam and
Jetsam of everyday,
Taking what we need
And leaving the rest.

In this age of down-sizing
We pare and peel away, shed
If you will, the layers of
Emotional skin, to which we are attached
But which serve us no longer.

We ask only that our Higher Power
Continue to accompany us, as we
Spiral upward toward our goal.
The Master Plan for which,
Each of us was created.
For only by staying the course,
Do we invite possibility.
And where possibility exists
So does success.

TEMPTATION

"Watch and pray, that ye enter
Not into temptation: the spirit
Indeed is willing, but the flesh
Is weak." Hebrew Scriptures.

As we enter upon the path of
Life, eyes moist from
Birth, unable to
Discern the direction
We are headed, many influences
Affect our decision.

If our early experience has
Taught us the concept of
Making do with less,
With that programmed into our psyche,
Along with being told
How redeeming a quality it is,
That will be
Our frame of reference.

Shying away from anything
That would require a financial
Investment, even if beneficial,
Would be a knee-jerk response,
Along with the glow of seeming
So sanctimonious, to those
Whose lives touch ours.

Does not our inability
To commit ourselves to
What is necessary to
Achieve the goal,
Speak in no uncertain terms
Of selling ourselves short?

The temptation to accept a
Lesser accommodation,
Relinquishing our needs more
Or less,
Inconveniencing ourselves
In the process, allowing the goal
To become that much harder to achieve,
Speaks of a major counterproductive
Mentality.

Accepting trade-offs disguised as
Glittering opportunities,
Holding them up to further
Scrutiny, finding no visible flaws,
Allowing ourselves then, to be enveloped
Within the folds of their promised
Appropriateness, ultimately falling short
Of the mark.

As well, as for instance,
Deciding to lower the curtain on a
Particular part of Life.
Acknowledging it's time, and
Being perfectly ready to do so.

But then, perhaps we are
Drawn inexorably
Back into the situation
As a result of an offer we
Couldn't refuse, or a massaged ego,
Or whatever the temptation.

Is it the offer
We couldn't refuse?
Or the compliment thrown our way
Like a rose at our feet,
Turning our heads 180 degrees?

Little red flags
Waving furiously,
Are not seen,
The glitter, so
Tantalizing.
Changes are then made
In the initial plan
Assuring us of our
Cleverness, our wisdom in the
Underlying situation.
Buying it.

Soon, if we are lucky,
A sense of un-comfortableness
Will occur, causing us moments
Of anxiety and resentment.
Lashing out at others perhaps,
For seeming actions on their
Part that wound or cause
Us uncomfortable feelings which truly
May have nothing to do with our
Discomfort.

Careful examination is required.
For it may be none of the above.
So often what seems to be the cause
Of our pain, comes from another
Source entirely.

The confusion and
Resentment, may be due to the
Inappropriate choices we made
For ourselves.
When the head finally figures
Out what the heart knew all
Along.
For if those two barometers are not
In sync there most assuredly will
Be moments of distress.

If we are blessed with the
Gift of awareness,
We are then given the chance
To make the
Necessary corrections.
Hopefully in time.

Going along with scenarios
Seemingly in our best interest,
Where there is no cost involved
Can be a heavy price to pay.
Perhaps requiring us to relinquish
Essential ideas sacred to
Our psyche thus opening the
Door to anger and guilt that could
Have been so easily avoided.

Remember,
There is a part of us
That really knows how
Deserving we are.
How long we have waited
To tap into the abundance
Of the Universe.
What it will take
To soothe our hearts, and
Nurture our souls.
Not putting roadblocks in the
Way of our success.
But rather stepping stones,
Recognizing that to accomplish the deed is
Difficult enough without
Adding to the angst.

But old convictions die hard.
As was said, this is a core
Issue.
Stories told in
The cradle as it were,
By those whose opinions we
Hold as sacrosanct.

Time to move on, to
A healthier outlook.
To refuse to accept less
Than the best.

There is some comfort
In old behavior.
That however, does not make it healthy.
Truly being in harmony with ourselves

Means simply, that we no longer accumulate
Outdated bundles of information,
Continuing to utilize them as
Rules to live by.

Rather,
To do our very best each day by
Treating ourselves and those around us
In ways second to none.
Disallowing temptation to send
Us spiraling downward, keeping in
Mind always, where we need to be.
The Higher Plane, enjoying
All of the benefits that will provide.

Saving for a rainy day
Most assuredly has its merits,
But can signal for some of us
The need to hold back in
What might indeed be a very
Gratifying moment.

And if we truly
Live in the moment it is
An opportunity never
Retrieved.
A little thought is needed
Here, rather than a spontaneous
Action.
It doesn't matter what the
First response may be.
As long as it is not acted upon.
Take the time to consider all
The variables.

Then go within,
To that sacred
Holy of Holies, your
Heart.
And in the ocean of silence
Float the possibilities
To consider.

In a very short time one
Answer will rise to the surface.
The right one.
It will feel that way from the
Very start, and temptation
Will have absolutely nothing
To do with it.

It will meet every need,
And have the ring of God's
Will about it, with the
Knowledge that if ignored,
The only temptation will be
Of the fates.

Rest then, in the knowledge
That you were able to
Heed that still small voice,
And more than that, recognize
It for what it was, a clarion
Call to do the next right thing.
Remember, next time it will be
Easier.

And so it is.

ENOUGH IS A FEAST

What is enough of anything?
The answer for anyone
Compulsive, is that "the amount has not
Yet been established."
With things that taste good,
And leave one with warm fuzzy
Feelings, *all* of it is not
Enough.

In relationships, when the
People I love are close about,
I become consumed in thinking of
When I will see them again, which
Plays in my head over and over,
Totally ignoring the joy
Of the moment.

I believe that this
Kind of thought process can
Place a great deal of pressure
On those whose company I do so
Enjoy.

Our children, truly delightful
To have around, may, with this kind
Of behavior on my part, misconstrue
The message, that having them near
Is totally necessary in order
For me to feel complete, placing
A mantle of distress upon their shoulders
That they most definitely would not
Choose to wear.
With my friendships, I fear that this
Kind of demeanor, which expresses
Such neediness, produces in them,
The urgency to back away.

We all need space.
This I understand intellectually.
Having breezes and light, blow through
Our lives, allows us to grow,
Outside of each others' shadow.

The healthy mind honors not only
Boundaries, but is able to place
Limitations on everything.
A positive lesson on
What to do to make
My world spin.
Which will usher in the
Satisfaction that
Comes from knowing I
Did what was necessary, while
Relinquishing the need for anyone
To be the commodity,
Without which I cannot
Fly.

How much more delightful then
It will be to dance to my own tune, to
Set my own course, knowing that
I have within all I need to follow it
Through to the end, solo if need be.

It then becomes imperative to
Excise the feeling
Of inadequacy.
Forsaking totally the need
For the crutch of familial support,
Which often only provides
False comfort.

For as I mature
I see and feel the need to
Be there for my family
As a parent,
Less and less often.

Early days spent
Beside the cradle,
Guiding first steps,
Holding small hands across dangerous
Thoroughfares, with
Caring watchful glances leaves me
Hopeful, that in passing
On Life's Rules to live by, I have
Dotted all the I's and crossed all the
T's.
Enough.

But what shows up in the final
Analysis, is not so much what
I said, about anything, but
What I did about everything.
That is what flies in
The face of all I have
Tried to get across.

What those who are the
Silent witnesses to my life will
Come away with.
Concepts that either hold water,
Or empty words which do not.

Added to this mix of
What I feel is important
To pass on, is what they
Have been sent here to accomplish
This lifetime.
And that is a contract strictly
Between themselves and who I
Choose to call God.
Signed and sealed at birth.
My gentle urgings, which proffer
Civility, and appropriate
Behavior, will ultimately be
Fashioned into a garment of
Their own making.
Theirs and God's.

Knowing this to be true
Along with letting go of the
Need for more, is an
Exhilarating feeling for
The accomplishment is so much
More delectable having been
Done in spite of powerful
Feelings to the contrary.

Did those first inhabitants of Eden,
Appreciate Paradise for what it was?
Maybe.
For a short while anyway.
For I believe, there was within
Themselves a degree of restlessness,
Which allowed temptation to seep through
The cracks of complacency,
The same old, same old,
Wore thin, pushing them toward
Whispered invitations.
The need for more.

Day after day of warm sunshine,
Adequate food, and drink, passing
The time with a loving companion,
With an absence of rough edges,
Was not enough.
Something cried out for them
To know more and have more.

The Tree of Life had so
Many branches.
Some had already flowered
And bore fruit, others with leaves
Barely visible, in their pale
Green suppleness, ushered in
The excitement of promise.

It was then that they became conscious
Of what was, but better yet
What was possible.
While living in the moment
Became a challenge.
Reflection and anticipation were then
Brought kicking and screaming onto
The scene.

Burnished to a high gleam,
The concept of the days
Ahead took on a heady quality
While the present moment was
Measured only in synthetic
Warmth.

Yes, the future brought with
It its own excitement.
The admonition to accept
What they already had as
Sufficient, was cast aside.
Whispered messages of more,
Pushed the button of
Temptation.

Today words like ubiquitous
Consumption, along with
Concepts such as less being
More, fly in the face of those
Like myself, who see some of
That as major deprivation.

Maybe then, what needs to be looked
At here are entitlements.
Yes, we are entitled to much.
All that the world has to offer.
And so is everyone else.
I don't feel that I am here
To wear it out, use it up, at
The expense of someone else.
Being satisfied sounds reasonable.
Recognizing that, is
Even better.
Being able to share with
Others is a big part of the
Equation.
But knowing when enough
Is enough is really where
It's at, because enough is a feast.

LIFE BY DEGREES

How we see the world and
The role we play in it,
May be based for the most part,
On what we do with our time,
Along with the experiences
Exacted upon us.

Sharing, that her husband's work,
Involving the use of a microscope,
Causes him to focus on details, that most
Others would never see,
My friend complained that he,
Because of being immersed in the world of minutia,
Loses sight of the bigger picture.
And may not even realize there *is* a
Bigger picture.

He has become nitpicky, obsessed
With details, while ignoring errors
Of judgment, social gaffes that
Beg correction, along with crass
Behavior, becoming very difficult
To live with.

How often do we, in the throes of dealing with
Something someone has said, latch onto a word or
Remark that has made us uncomfortable, or
Opened up an area of discontent, rendering us
Incapable of dealing with it rationally?
Causing us to spend an inordinate amount
Time focused on it.

Ruminating over the impediment
Until it becomes all consuming, a
Minor detail, becoming larger
Than life, dwarfing everything
In its path.

Not really a different concept, just manifest
In a different way, with similar results.
Any artist can tell you that
Looking too closely at anything for
Long periods of time, reduces our
Capacity to take in the overall
Design.
We need to step back.

Concentration that is so
Dedicated and focused on any one
Thought or idea for an inordinate
Amount of time causes our
Vision to be restricted, reduced
To the very finite.
With the consideration of other
Matters to just not
Be there.

Also impaired may be our
Ability to hear the valid
Concerns of others, if we
Measure them against our
Much more exciting, painful,
Gut wrenching, or whatever
We feel, our life's experiences
To be by comparison.

As has been said before,
We are here to learn
Lessons, and depending on how
Many chances we have been
Given to work out a particular assignment,
Our awareness of our part in it,
Along with our ability to
Recognize the right answer
Will determine our coming up
With a solution.
The best part of that being,
Once mastered, it will never have to be repeated
Throughout all eternity.
How motivating is that?

But before we get carried away
With looking at the entire canvas,
We need to bring some order to the chaotic
Ways in which we think,
Done best by going at it
One day at a time, one step at
A time, establishing the
Path of a well-ordered life.

Readjusting our lens so that
We are able to download
The whole picture into our
Frame of reference.

A life lived by degrees.

PASS IT ON

A long, dark corridor ushers in the receding
Images of my life, where they appear in
Sharp focus, and full color.

I strain to see it all in detail,
But the day to days,
Now relegated to tape,
Play only
When triggered by like circumstance,
And when the lesson is not learned.
Mastery of the task, ends
The repetition.

Suddenly, the miracles of my life
Occur at speeds so accelerated they
Tumble one over the other
As headwaters, spilling over polished
Stones, rendering one giddy with the
Experience.

Seeing these Divine Interventions, I
View the world, as one huge, transparent globe,
Whose inner workings fall efficiently,
And quietly into place.

There have been major shifts for me,
Logistically and
In other ways as well.
The quest for things has slowed.
But the voyage within has deepened.

Taking myself with me wherever I go,
Requires a traveling companion . . . a
Higher Self, who speaks the language
Of comfort, employing gentle, soft
Words to nurture, as I am led through
Days with rough edges, and dark valleys,
Flooded with waters of indecision and
Confusion.

Antiquated solutions often accompany me
Into new experiences.
Familiar methods, none of which
Are suited to take me the rest of the way.
Yet, there is solace in looking back
To times when I was taken cared of, my needs
Met by those responsible for my survival.

Eventually, through agonizingly slow
Realizations, or with a shock or a sudden
Jolt, I become aware of changes . . .
The game of hide and seek has
Come full circle . . . and now I am It.
Having to do for myself,
That which had always
Been done for me.

Some of us never get to
That place of self-sufficiency,
Where we gracefully assume the
Role of parent, instinctively
Knowing when, how, and what to do
To make ourselves function
At the highest level possible.

Slipping into the cloak of Maturity
Can for some, be as easy as brushing
Away a tear, or smiling at one's
Reflection in the mirror.
For me, donning the garment of
Sophistication, has been accompanied with
Much tugging and grappling, with
The loose ends of childhood
Flying all about.

Done reluctantly may be another
Way of putting it. I was always one
Who anticipated the future, no matter
What age I was at the time,
Always wondering what I would be
When I grew up.

In some ways, that can be a
Very healthy way of looking
At life. Childlike . . . as
Opposed to being childish.
However, this can also lead
To disappointment with the moment,
Throwing it aside for concepts or
Ideas, fledgling in their development,
Barely off the ground, blocking
The gift of the here and now.

Sparks of spontaneity
Are necessary to
Generate the Wheel of Circumstance,
Spinning where it will . . . we need
All the readiness at our command
To grab the brass ring . . . remembering
That ready or not
Here it comes . . .

And there it goes . . . waiting for
Our lives to be perfect before
Enjoying it is a mistake . . .
Carrying with it a very high price.
For each moment affords an
Opportunity, once gone . . .
Never retrieved.
Utilizing each one to best
Advantage, becomes a
Herculean task that cannot
Be done alone.

We need to be mindful of
Who is in charge, and in the
Simplest manner, ask for His
Guidance to be shown, What
Is his wish for us?
Only in this way can our lives
Make sense, ultimately allowing
Us to fashion a tapestry not only
Uniquely beautiful, but meaningful
As well.

For life, to me, comprises
More than images, and must, if
It is to be one of value, incorporate
The fulfillment of God's plan
For me . . . Actions. Yes, they do speak
Far louder than words. Putting into
Play all manner of deeds that say about
Us, far more than we could ever
Say about ourselves.

The candles burn low . . .
Our season of accomplishment
Is on the wane . . . no time
For judgments or
Recriminations . . . do the deed.

Hoping that our images,
Reflected by those candles
Will be straight and tall . . .
Reaching out beyond ourselves . . . and
Touching those who need most
What we have to give.
Hoard nothing.
Hide not, your light under a barrel.
God's precious gifts wither,
And the sin, mortal or not,
Lies in under-utilization . . .
Use them up.
Like manna, the supply is
Endless, freshly delivered
Each day.
We are renewed . . .
But with the renewal comes the
Proviso . . . to care,
To give back, to tithe, to pass it on.
We must not waste those
Gifts that are unique
To ourselves, that God so
Graciously has draped across our
Shoulders, the mantle of Providence.

Casting shadows on the
Barricades, put there
To protect us from unwanted
Influences from without,
Beckon us now, to
Hasten their removal . . .
For as they keep at bay,
That which would be harmful,
They also prevent us from
Fully experiencing the joys
That are our just rewards.

We need to step forward
With all the courage we can
Muster . . . Breathe in deeply the
Air of compassion . . . replace
The Image of Self, with that of
Higher Being . . . and mete out to
Those in need, that which has been
Given to us . . . and in the
Full bloom of generosity
Pass it on . . .
Pass it on . . .
Pass it on.

> "They will forget what you said.
> They will forget what you did.
> But they will never forget how you made them feel."
> —Anonymous

FEELINGS WE LIVE BY

To this very day, many of us given
Certain scenarios, react with
Responses that come from
Another time and place.

The doors to our attics
Swing wide,
Offering up all manner of
Postures, attitudes and opinions
Stated as fact, and so deeply
Ingrained, we don't see
Them for what they are.
Gospel fed to very small children.

Those children still exist, albeit
No longer visible
But definitely present,
Along with one hundred percent recall.
We can on occasion recite the "stuff"
Of which our lives were made
Book, Chapter and Verse.

In that inner world it matters not
How accurate the information,
Appropriate for the time, or
How often it has been

Proven to be false.

It rears its ugly head time
And time again not only
Verbatim, but with the same
Inflection and delivery as
At its initial offering.

Repeating these thoughts
Of "gold" to others
Who by choice can take what
They need and leave the rest
Is one thing, but spouting
The dictum
Over and over, to the hardened
Once sensitive ears of our inner child
Rendered useless ages ago, in its
Ability to filter out its inappropriateness
Is futile in itself.

It is a prescribed response that
We have fallen heir to.
Grown callous in our youth,
Our rhetoric also speaks
Of our inability
To comprehend its impact.

Abrupt remarks tumble from our
Mouths, and with no
Discriminating ear we are
Unable to stem its flow.

Looks, puzzled or hurt often follow,
Causing us to cringe along with
An immediate apology, often
An ongoing story line.

Ah, but when the mirror is in place
And we are able to juxtapose
Positions with those whose
Souls have felt the heat of those remarks,
Ours crumble.

It is then too late,
Words flung out, cannot
Be caught, erased, swallowed
Or obliterated in any way.
They become instant
Boomerangs, Karma . . .

Is it really necessary to tell
It like it is?
What is the gain in shooting from the hip?
Giving opinions without being
Asked?
Is being in control worth the price?
What is the benefit in having
A spin on someone else's
Life, while struggling so with
Our own?

When in this mode
We can be clueless as to
How diminishing it is,
And how much pain it causes.

But, aware of it or not,
It does.
Embarrassment, shame, guilt
Erupt full-blown in the
Exchange.

We need to remember
It is by the
Grace of God, special people
Are brought into our lives, our
Paths crossing on the journey being
No small miracle, and
Never by accident.

That the people with whom we
Deal on this plane have unique
Personal attributes, but much more
Than that, they have a Spirit
Radiating far beyond what is visible.

When inappropriate things are said,
Inappropriate gestures made,
No gift on Earth can heal the wounds, or
Bind the injured Soul.

If the injury is inflicted on
A child, often the perception of the
Words spoken, along with the crushed Spirit
Remain in that state long after the
Assault, to be played
Back intermittently throughout
Their lives.

Such an odd legacy to
Leave behind, and yet so many
Do this very thing over and over
Again without the realization

That they will be forever associated
With the pain, shame and guilt manifest
On someone ill-equipped to protect
Themselves.

Opinions thrust in the face of
Another, often result in feelings
Of low self-esteem made even more
Painful when the messenger is
Someone looked upon with much respect.
How sad that in so many instances
That respect is grossly overrated.

The trinkets that were given
Will be left by the roadside.
Our accomplishments of this lifetime, will
Be over-shadowed by theirs . . .
What will remain however when they
Think of us, are the feelings.
Will they be the warm, rosy glow of
A nurturing and comforting Soul,
Or of someone who left holes in
Their fabric, causing their integrity
And self-image to leach out,
Becoming less than,
Perhaps forever?

While there is still time, we
Must do what we can to stitch up
Those gaps eaten away by the acid
Of thoughtless moments.

And instead fill them with the
Sweetly fragrant blossoms
Of appreciation,
That they are here,
That they are special,
That they give much
Joy, Love and Meaning to our lives, and
That they occupy a special place in our
Hearts forever.

That is when their less than
Whole selves will knit
Into completeness, allowing them to
Step out into the world,
A unit, altogether sound.
Knowing that they are
Beloved children of God,
Ready and capable to do God's Will.
And that they are endowed
With all they will ever need,
And that it is good.
So be it!

FORTY YEARS TOO LATE

Brushing up against the Wheel of Fortune
Probably more times than I can remember, I
Chose to walk the narrow road that had been
Charted for me genetically and experientially.

I allowed the opportunities that could
Have, would have, should have been, to slip
Quietly, almost unnoticed through my fingers.
No room in my world for choices
Other than the obvious.
At least obvious to me.

We had ushered two new souls
Into the world, whose direction
And focus needed a caring, loving
Hand.
One that would be a constant in
An otherwise rudderless and sometimes
Scary place.

There have always been
Moments, if not centuries,
Of violence, coupled with
Temptations of the soul,
Weakness of Spirit,
And weariness of heart,
To have coaxed those with little strength
Down the primrose path,
Causing them to fall,
Not only short of their potential,
But often from Grace altogether.

It could be said that all of
Our experiences are God's will.
But that would omit our power to choose.
Deciding, when facing a fork
In the road, which one
Suits us best.

If not led by someone with a very
Long leash, we may lack the
Confidence that comes with being
Allowed to take chances
Making decisions early.
Creating mistakes then, lessens the chances
That the consequences will be dire,
The lessons formidable.

Learning to listen to our own heartbeat,
Recognizing it as such, along with
Witnessing the glow of our own inner candle,
Often ushers in a lifetime of fulfillment.

Sometimes in the busy world of doing and giving
To others, our bliss, if recognized
At all, is put on the back burner in
Order to honor those priorities.
Losing sight of the here and now as it
Relates to ourselves, allows precious
Moments to slip away.
Once gone, never retrieved.
Denying totally the immediacy of
The moment, we forget that our
Bliss, may not be powerful, or
Potent enough to sit quietly
By, remaining fresh and unaltered.
On the contrary it may become old,
Or wither away completely.

There is no sign upon our brow warning
Us of the diminution of our talent if
Not used within a given time.
But whether there is or not, the
Truth is, it does.
And if unused, how unrealistic is it
For us to expect it to remain fresh and
Vital, while hidden from the light of
Day, and from the inner
Promptings of the
Soul?
Totally.

For as surely as we can attest to the
Passage of time, we will awaken one day,
To find the service and work that took
Precedence over it all,
Done.
Those in our care have moved on.
Do we then turn within to address that
Part of ourselves put on hold,
Expecting it to be there intact?
Some of us do.

Only to find it is too late.
The role suited to the ingenue is
No longer appropriate.
The lilt in the voice, the
Dance in our step, relegated now only
To the mind's eye, or light in the
Soul.
Totally delusional.
Rip Van Winkle revisited.
We have awakened to find the dream
Is present, without form and
Substance.

Yet, the flame of desire so long
On simmer, may ignite into a roaring
Blaze, but without the tinder to
Feed the flame, it will most assuredly
Sputter and die.

Acceptance is the answer.
Coming to terms with the
Statement that "What is, is
What ain't, ain't.
Going beyond believing, to
Knowing I am forty years too late.

SHADOWS ON THE WALL

Not all discoveries made
In life come to us struggle-free.
Many are accompanied by dark nights
Of the Soul.
At times there is justification
Solid, viable, and blinding
That speak volumes
For the actions taken.

Most recently this was
The case,
Concerning an issue in
My life that was incomplete.
Not realizing that at the
Time though, we relocated
Ourselves, leaving not
Only the area, but the
Opportunities that would
Have enabled me to correct
That deficit.

What was undone was not
Large in any sense,
But, something I felt
I deserved and
After all,
I was still viable and more than capable and

It would bring closure to a
Part of my life, allowing me
To exit stage right, with a song
In my heart, knowing that my
Goal had been met.

Obsessing over its absence
Ate holes in my shield of
Acceptance and serenity causing me to lose
Sight of the gifts
Already in hand.

People were quick to agree and
Ably followed the lines
I painted in so
Freely.
It was I who chose the colors,
No right or wrong there,
Just my choice, and so
The Quest began.
With one caveat,
Established by me.
A time limit.
Ignoring the concept
Of my time vs. God's time,
I decreed when I would
Start and when it would be over.
Unequivocally.

I then returned to the place where
It all began, and tried
With the help of others, to
Fill the gap.
Mend the hole.
Finish the job.
I went back three times.
Each time coming close
But not close enough.

The last time, dark days began to
Overshadow the glow of
Excitement that only possibilities
Provide.
Those, very slow in coming.

Suiting up and showing up?
My responsibility.
Everything else was out of my hands.

Along with the dim view
That permeated my days,
There was fear.
Fear that my time frame might
Have been somewhat unrealistic.
But then came the first phone call.
Sending me out to show what
I could do.
This scenario always followed
By waiting, is never easy for someone
With a low threshold of patience.
Along with the euphoria
That comes with the feelings of
Thinking I did well, was also the angst of
Would I hear?
Would I get it?
If so, when?

All this made for a very stressful existence.
My self-imposed deadline
Edged closer.
The tossing and turning began.
For with each successive
Opportunity the carrot moved
Further down the time line.

For if I was in contention,
With the need to be seen twice,
I would have to be there even if it
Went beyond my limited stay.
How could I leave before I
Knew whether this was it?

What began to wreak
Havoc with my emotional
Equilibrium, was the vision
Of never being able to go
Home.
That this one room, which
Held me captive, would be
Where I would ultimately be,
In perpetuity.

It was then the spin began.
And spin it did.
Around and around
Over and over,
Blocking out any glimmer of
Light, or sanity.
Spinning a web in the dark.
No answers come in the dark.
At least none that are clear.
The fighting is all consuming.
What am I fighting?
Shadows on the wall?

Certainly nothing I can see.
No bird in the hand.
Everything hidden in the
Bush.
Old saws came to
Mind accelerating the spin.
Hysteria followed.
I reached out to others, in
Order to give voice to my
Panic in the hope of
Regaining calm
And focus.

I am then told that
"This would be the time to
Reach in for courage,
Courage to hold on.
To acknowledge how much of
That commodity it took to
Do this in the first place."
But how can I when it is so
Dark?
What covered the window
Of reason was the black shade
Of fear, the fear that
Without completing this
Quest I would lack comfort for
The rest of my journey, that
There would be no soft place to fall.
And just maybe my personae would
Not be accompanied by a recognizable
Tag of achievement.
When in reality I have that
And more.

With almost fifty years of my life
Shared with one who gives comfort
And support, along with children
And grandchildren whose love and
Respect is palpable,
I am truly wealthy.
I have friends who share their vision
Of the mountain with me, in a warm and
Gentle part of the Universe.

And above all I am guided through
Each day by a God who knows me better
Than I know myself, who is definitely
In charge, and through whom all my
Needs will be met.
All my needs.
Forever.

I can finally see that
The most challenging aspect of my life
Is staying in that trust
And love.
But
There are so many ways I am
Tempted not to do so, so many
Voices calling from outside
Telling me to fear—
That I won't be okay, that I
Won't be safe, that I won't
Have enough.
When in fact, if that trust is in place,
Fear cannot be.

A prayer steals quietly into this
Wilted Spirit.
A magnificent truth,
Painted broadly.
In strokes so pure in color, and
Vivid that I cannot help but see
What was so
Indistinguishable in
The dark-clouded moments just
A short time before, yes they
Were shadows.
Shadows on the wall.
Nothing more,
Nothing less.
Shadows on the wall.
Evaporating immediately
With the realization that
If God had this plan in mind
For me nothing this side of
Heaven and Earth would prevent it.
But that if I continued to try
To manipulate it into being, without it
Being His will, nothing this side of Heaven
And Earth would allow it to happen . . .

MEMORIES ARE BETTER

Memories are better than dreams my friend,
They are yours and are nestled within.
They belong to the one who has truly lived life,
With the courage it took to begin.

It's never been easy, to find what it was,
That nourished our souls, at the start.
But with focus, and trials, much searching and pain
We found the Gold Path to the heart.

And that's where it lies, it's the crux of it all,
The doorway that ushers in Truth,
And whenever we find it, be it early or late,
How much sweeter, if found in our youth.

For the time that is spent in pursuits
That are real, bring us such joy and delight
No material pleasures accrued on this Earth
Can compare, it's like day and night.

When we can connect with our Higher Self
And apply the advise that we're shown
Each day becomes special, emblazoned with Gold,
Far better than we've ever known.

The service we offer,
The help that we give
The messages we are to send,
Are all our agenda,
Our reason for being,
The real deal, and not just pretend.

When we look at it all
What the mind should recall
Is not how much time did it take,
But how well we performed all the
Tasks that we had, and was it all
Done for God's sake?

If we can say yes, to all the above
Then truly we've earned our Gold Star,
Along with a smile, and a warm sense of pride,
In being, who God said we are.

So keep asking for clarity
Strength and His will
To be shown to you
Twenty-four seven.
There will be no doubt
You'll have figured it out
You'll have fashioned on
Earth
Your own Heaven.

It's worth it you know
Whatever you do,
To walk with the sun in your face.
To follow your bliss, do what you do best
So much better than standing in
Place.

The smile that will come
Over all that you've done
Earning in God's world
A spot, says
In spite of it all
You answered the call
And showed up no matter what.

At the end of the road
You'll unburden your load
And surrender your struggles
And strife.
And your face it will glow
With what you now know,
Are reflections of
Your part in life.

You will shimmer and
Sparkle, and radiate
Far, and your gleam will
Survive ages long.
For you took what you got,
Be it less or a lot
And did just the best you knew how.
And the memories you've spun
From work that you've done
Are a Hymn to His name.
Do it now!

THE MIRROR GOT OLD

The skyscrapers stand as sentinels, gigantic
Forts guarding against those who come
To denigrate the city, by tearing apart
The very fabric of its essence.

The windows in these monuments
Open out on creativity of
Every variety.
Spinning minds provide
The pace, generating
The energy that
Is undeniably New York.

Being in contact with this
Vitality, this major life force, disallows
The age factor to enter into the equation,
As I concentrate on my intention.
I relegate it to the back burner,
Focusing only on the opportunity
Presented.

Steps quicken, along with the
Blood, rising to meet the rhythm of
The moment, taking into account
What is required to make the supreme
Effort necessary,
In order to succeed.

All this activity of the mind
Sends the message that this
Is real, and that here is a
Place to be
Taken seriously.

There are links here.
Connections, that once made,
Will stand the test of time . . .
Which however is the question.
Always moving,
Never waiting,
No holding it in place.

The child within, anxious to
Insure her place, loses track of
How long it has been, this quest
To fulfill her desire.

Locked within each of us is this
Sweet small voice,
Truly ageless,
In place, since our time
Here began.
Growing louder, as we become
Aware of following our bliss,
That whisper of the
Soul honoring
The contract made with our
Creator upon our arrival.
We think it will always be thus.
The striving, the need to move
Laterally, perhaps not realizing
That our offering may have lost
Its edge.

Is there a major sense of denial?
Do we miss, that with each step forward,
We leave a part of ourselves behind?
That with each experience we have,
It either enhances or diminishes
What it is we have
Going for us?
Time definitely the culprit here.

In preparation I get myself
Together, fashioning the image,
Known as "me."
Stepping out to meet the challenge
The child makes her move.
Failing to realize that the
Child is no more.
Somewhere between dawn and
Sunset she lost sight of
Who she was.

Acknowledging that reality
Is very hard.
I look upon myself with eyes
That have failed to mature
Along with the rest of me,
Having grown accustomed to seeing
Myself an ingénue, fledgling,
Becoming not having yet arrived.

Surprise, if not shock greets
Me, when someone
Taking note of my presence, offers me
Something I see as being reserved for
Someone more mature.
A seat on the bus!
Looking around, I find
It difficult to imagine that this
Kindness is being directed at me.
What prevents me from seeing
Who it is that I have become?
Is it my eyes that remain soft and
Eternally young?
Continuing to register loyalty in lieu
Of honesty to the reflection in the mirror?
Maybe so, but wait,
Of course, it's
The mirror . . .
It got old!

MUSICAL CHAIRS

Years go by, and on any given day
We may find ourselves
Nestled in family warmth and
Friendly persuasions.
Touching those with whom we built
The foundation of our lives.

The comfort we experience
Watching people doing
Familiar things, things for
Which they are known,
Is palpable.

And when living one's life
One day at a time,
No thought need be given
To changing the scenario
Because right here,
Right now, it is perfect.

Plans are made, based on
The fact that we are available.
Our friends have no other plans
They too are able to
Participate, and so we will call
At the end of the week to firm up
The arrangements.
"Hear from you then."

Except, something else comes in
To disrupt the anticipated event.
Something totally out of left field,
Not expected at all.

The friend is stricken.
Not able to make it, nor,
As it turns out, will he
Ever be.
On life support, yet based on
A prior arrangement made while in
The throes of living a busy life, he is
Removed from same, because
The idea of being alive sans all
Manner of recognizable trappings
Will not be acceptable.

The call is made to tell
Those whose lives touched his,
About the funeral, when
And where.
So many thoughts enter our minds.
The immediate gratitude
That we have dodged the bullet, followed
With much reticence
In being witness to the
Event, but respect begs
Participation.

It is, as we arrive that
The familiarity of the scene
Takes over.
Signing the book in the
Foyer.
Greeting the family with all
The appropriate messages of comfort.
Finding a seat in the sanctuary.
Preparing to hear more messages of
Comfort, this time spoken to
All.
Dealing with the speed at which the
Rock upon which our lives stood
Has been altered requires much
Concentration.
And if we were especially close to the person
Who left our midst, we then accompany
Him to his grave,
Where more familiarity enters our frame
Of reference.
Gathering with others
In small circles.
Close family,
People from the workplace,
Family who may have been at a distance
Until this moment, finds them
Filling each other in on what has happened
In their lives until today.
Neighbors who actually lived the day to
Days with the departed.
And then the finality that comes with the
Shovel full of dirt, hitting the
Coffin, and the hollow sound that is its
Accompaniment.

Once we reach a certain age,
With this scenario repeating itself again and again
We begin to see the drill,
See it for what it really is.
Preparation.
For as the parade comes closer, so
Do all the familiar posturing
And mental gymnastics.
It all begins to make sense.

None of it will be foreign.
We will have been through it all
Countless times before.
Except there will come a time and
This we can count on, that we will
Definitely be in a different chair.
Perhaps we will be the one
Who is being reassured
By the messages of others,
Sitting directly inside the foyer, whose
Hands are grasped while gazing into the eyes
Of those paying their respects.
Soft quiet voices, accompanied
By glances barely hitting their mark.
Not glances that are glazed over with
Indifference . . . not this time . . .
No, rather looks that have the air
Of discomfort, realizing that for the moment,
Truly, just for the moment,
They are not
In your chair.

And with each of these gatherings
We will feel the parade edging closer and closer
Knowing that at any time,
The game of musical chairs, will accelerate
And that the day will come,
When we will have run out of chairs,
Our vantage point having passed that
Stage, having moved on.
So,

May we spend each day until that moment
In pursuits that are worthwhile,
Necessary, and filled to
Overflowing with joy.
The joy of doing His will,
Knowing completely that this really is
All there is.

THE NEED TO SAY GOOD-BYE

Beginnings are important.
The way we attack a project.
How we prepare for any contingency.
Making sure that all avenues are
Investigated, along with the
Discussions necessary in getting
The project off the ground.
Courage too, is essential in
Taking the first step.

This is true in relationships as well.
None of us can be that sure of our
Footing when it comes to unknown
Territory.
How comforting then to have someone
With whom you can share ideas, your
Plans, whether at the deepest philosophical
Level, or while engaging in banter of the
Most whimsical sort.
It allows for other perspectives,
Views from the bridge different from our own.

When considering a journey to a new place
Maps are consulted as well as friends who
May have found their way to where you are
Headed.

Along with mapping out the adventure, the
Reasons for going are mentioned, allowing
The experience to be shared on a much more
Intimate level.

This is not just for the pleasure of the
Anticipated event, but because in the
Give and take of the moment, those with whom
We are in contact have an investment in the
Occurrence, and can look forward with eager
Anticipation to its taking place, as well
As to its outcome.

Why then in Heaven's name, with the advent
Of one's final journey on the horizon, would
One opt to go quietly into the night,
Without so much as a whisper, without the
Benefit of light from the countless candles
Ready, willing and able to shine their way
Into our hearts and onto our path?

This would be the last comparative.
The final opportunity to go over our
Life's experience.
To investigate for the last time
The accuracy of the lessons learned.
Checking others' answers to the questions
That have plagued us for so long.
Perhaps coming away with the reassurance
And joy that we were right on target and
Had passed that part of Life with flying
Colors.
Or, and sometimes not until the very last
Moment, do we recognize the real answer,
An automatic guarantee of our never having
To repeat this challenge throughout
Eternity.
Such a comfort.

But walking through that dark tunnel
Alone, affords us nothing of the kind.
For no matter the length of our days
We deserve companionship to see us
On our way.
A warm hand to hold, other than that
Of our Higher Power, a friend or loved
One to whom we have been connected.
Someone to wish us Bon Voyage, to
Walk us out, to sing us over.
To tell our story, with us as silent
Witness, reminding us of who we are
And were to so many.
Thus meeting both our needs and that of
Closure.
The need to say good-bye.

SEPTEMBER ELEVENTH
TWO THOUSAND ONE

The shrill winds of havoc blew through here today,
And thousands of lives did succumb.
With horrified gaze we watched evil at play
Until all of our senses were numb.

Explosively fashioned with huge bursts of fire,
Broken bones, hearts, and spirits moist
With tears,
Steel, tangled and twisted, shards of
Glass, and fine dust, playing into
A person's worst fears.

What would you do ninety floors in the air
Surrounded with fire at your heels?
The choices, not many, do you burn, do you jump?
Too frightening to think of.
They were there.

Holding hands they let go, taking wing
Through the sky, while screaming so loud
With one voice.
A decision so painful, too painful to bear,
But then as I said, not much choice.

Clouds roiling through alleys
Enormous and black, spilling over,
Among and within.
Panic, hearts racing, the need to get out,
Retribution?
Yeah . . .
But for what sin?

There were some who were stuck
Through no fault of their own,
Deserted by worker and staff,
One, in a wheelchair lifting
Prayers to on High,
When two angels appeared, wings full blown.

It was floor sixty-eight, where they
Happened to see
Her sitting alone in the gloom.
With no time to waste they
Grabbed hold of the chair, they
Could not let her die in that tomb.

With step after step they
Made the descent, not thinking
Of aught but just that,
With chest aching, legs tight
And their eye on the goal they
Kept on, no time to fall flat.

They made it miraculously, with
No time to spare,
Smothered in dust and debris,
Down in the street, firefighters rushed past
To the stairs, up
To their destiny.

The building caved in
In huge ruffles of
Smoke, one rode it
Right down to the ground.
But thousands of others
Caught up in the fumes,
Disappeared, and would never
Be found.

Name upon name etched
Into the steel as
It melted and twisted about.
Then ever so silently, wave upon wave
The souls lifted, were raised
And were out.

I heard someone say a
Long time ago,
Describing just what is insane . . .
Repeating behavior
Expecting different results . . .
Well, we only have ourselves to blame.

As a country, a people,
We need to own up
To the things that we've done
Gone awry.
Things done with intention
Both good and both bad
Where others were killed
Wondering why.

Until we can do that,
Can come face to face,
With what didn't work in
Our past,
Until we can say we won't do
It again,
Until we can write a new script,
We'll be open to others
Getting payback and such
With periods of peace that
Won't last.

So what do you say we make our amends
Turning over a brand new page?
Where all our intentions are good,
And none bad, and all of our
Wisdom is sage.

We will truly have won both
The battle and war, while to
Ourselves being true, we'll walk a path
Narrow,
Our eye on His will
With only goodness and mercy
Shining through.

Amen.

BVG

Take a Praise Break:
Celebrate the Works of God!

Marilyn E. Thornton
Abingdon Press

CONTENTS

Introduction 3

Lesson One
    Praise God For Freedom 4

Lesson Two
    The Faith To Pray 12

Lesson Three
    The Savior's Birth 20

Lesson Four
    Lost And Found 27

Lesson Five
    Marching To Zion 34

Introduction

Even as it may seem as though many of the gains in civil and human rights accomplished over the years have slipped away, it is always good to take time to stop and praise the Lord and to acknowledge that God has brought us from a mighty long way! That's what the Hebrew children did when they got away from the Egyptians (Exodus 14:31-15:2, 20-21). That's what Hezekiah did when he got word that he would be healed (Isaiah 38:1-5, 9, 19-21). The angels stopped to praise God after announcing the birth of Jesus (Luke 2:8-15) and Jesus said that the rocks would cry out if the people stopped praising God (Mark 11:7-9; Luke 19:39-40). When the woman found her lost coin, she got her friends together and they celebrated (Luke 15:8-10). Following their example, in many African American churches, there are points in worship wherein a testimony, a song, or a sermon is just so good that it calls for a "praise break": a spontaneous prayer, an unscheduled song, a holy dance, or just hands lifted in praise and thanksgiving! And that's what this program is all about, celebrating and stopping to praise God for how God is working in our individual lives and in the life of the people. As the overall Scripture suggests, those who have been saved from any kind of trouble should testify about it.

"Let the redeemed of the LORD say so . . ." (Psalm 107:2a NRSV)!

The writer for *Take a Praise Break: Celebrate the Works of God* is the Rev. Marilyn E. Thornton, who has formulated curriculum programs that utilize African American history and culture as a springboard at Abingdon Press for eleven years. She is a preacher, musician, storyteller, and educator, who loves to share the story of God's salvation for all people, using various media. Even as she developed the entire program of which this Bible study is a part, it is a special blessing and a privilege for Rev. Thornton to be the exclusive writer for this component. Upon concluding this study, she hopes that each participant will be ready to "Let the redeemed of the LORD say so," take a praise break and celebrate the works of God!

LESSON 1

PRAISE GOD FOR FREEDOM

Exodus 14:31-15:2

Key Verse
This is my God, whom I will praise, the God of my ancestors, whom I will acclaim. (Exodus 15:2b)

Opening Prayer
O God, Our Rescuer!
You, alone, have the power to save. From the beginning, you have brought us through many trials and we can trust in you for continued help. Empower us to share about your overflowing victories that others may claim you as their God. In Jesus' name. Amen.

Bible Lesson

14:31 Israel saw the amazing power of the LORD against the Egyptians. The people were in awe of the LORD, and they believed in the LORD and in his servant Moses. 15:1 Then Moses and the Israelites sang this song to the LORD:

  I will sing to the LORD,
    for an overflowing victory!
    Horse and rider he threw into the sea!
2 The LORD is my strength and my power;
    he has become my salvation.
  This is my God, whom I will praise,
      the God of my ancestors,
      whom I will acclaim.

20 Then the prophet Miriam, Aaron's sister, took a tambourine in her hand. All the women followed her playing tambourines and dancing. 21 Miriam sang the refrain back to them:
    Sing to the LORD,
      for an overflowing victory!
      Horse and rider he threw into the sea!

It's Time

The year 2013 marked the 150th anniversary of the signing of the Emancipation Proclamation (1863), wherein President Abraham Lincoln declared all persons held as slaves in the regions of rebellion to be free! This proclamation came way too late for Frederick Douglass (c.1818-1895), who by 1838 traveled by foot, boarded two trains and two boats to leave slavery in Maryland and gain freedom in Philadelphia, Pennsylvania! Douglass traveled to freedom over the waters of the Susquehanna, Christina and Delaware Rivers while the Hebrew children walked on a path of dry land through the waters of the Red Sea. Both journeys represent the power of God to save and to empower escape from oppression into freedom! Knowing about God's delivering power should make you want to take a praise break and celebrate how God works, whether in ancient Egypt or in the United States of America.

The Back Story

The story of the escape of the Israelites from slavery in Egypt to a land of freedom is foundational to the identity of not only people of Judeo-Christian faith but also to many African Americans, who identified with God who frees rather than one who endorsed enslavement. The story is told in song.

When Israel was in Egypt land; let my people go!
Oppressed so hard they could not stand; let my people go!
Go down Moses, way down in Egypt Land
Tell ol' Pharaoh to let my people go!

God told the Israelites to never forget, how they had been freed and that God had done it.

"This day shall be a day of remembering for you. You will observe it as a festival to the LORD. You will observe it in every generation as a regulation for all time." (Exodus 12:14)

They were to rehearse their freedom story once a year, at Passover. That story has become the backdrop for the holy meal, of which Christians partake to celebrate what Christ did in delivering humanity from slavery to sin into the freedom of life with Christ. The Hebrews ate the very first Passover meal of unleavened bread and roasted lamb as an angel passed over their homes. The doorposts and lintels of their homes had been painted with the blood of that lamb. This identified them as Hebrews. The homes of the Egyptians had not been painted and so each one experienced the death of the first-born. This constituted the tenth plague announced by Moses in God's campaign to convince the Egyptians to free the enslaved Israelites peaceably.

Two quotes by Frederick Douglass thousands of years later vividly describe the situation faced by both the Hebrews in Egypt and Blacks in American oppression.

> *"Power concedes nothing without a demand. It never did and it never will."*
>
> *"It is not light that we need, but fire; it is not the gentle shower, but thunder. We need the storm, the whirlwind, and the earthquake."*

So God sent a storm of death so that power would concede and upon discovery of a deceased loved one in their homes the following morning, the Egyptians sent the Hebrew slaves away to follow their destiny.

But they changed their minds! They said, "What!? Where are my biscuits? Who is going to change the baby's diapers? It's cotton chopping time!" Pharaoh gathered an army, outfitted with chariots and horses and trained officers, to pursue the Israelites all the way to the edge of the wilderness. The Hebrew children looked back and saw that the Egyptians were gaining ground; they looked in front and saw the Red Sea and they turned to Moses saying, "What have you done? We told you to leave us alone (Exodus 14:11-12)!" As directed by God, Moses lifted his staff and stretched his hand over the water. An east wind blew in, separating the water into walls on either side of a dry path through which the Hebrews escaped to the other shore. And when the Egyptians tried to follow, the walls of water came tumblin' down and the Egyptians drowned.

Discussion Questions
1. When did you first hear the Exodus story?
2. What do you know about Frederick Douglass?

Changing One's Mind (Exodus 14:30-31)

Water is powerful! From Noah's flood to Hurricane Katrina, to tsunamis, humanity is aware of water's destructive power. Nevertheless, water is necessary for life; our bodies are at least 70 percent water. If we do not drink enough of it, we will have medical problems. One of the first things hospital personnel does for a patient is to give fluids. And yet excessive water is dangerous and God, whose Spirit swept over the waters at Creation (Genesis 1:2), knows this better than anyone. We may question why there have been so many water disasters in the world. Some like to claim them as punishment for sin or as being due to global warming. And while global warming did not exist during these ancient biblical times, we can certainly see that the Egyptians were operating in opposition to God, the very definition of sin.

God desires freedom for all people. God had communicated over and over that the Hebrew children should be freed from their enslavement to Egypt. The Egyptians had had many opportunities to get with the program and yet they refused until losing a loved one. Then they changed their minds! How true to human nature! We can know what is the right thing to do; yet we continually pursue that which is against God's purpose and design, that which seeks the common good. People often wonder why the same kinds of negative things keep happening to them. Often it is because they have not learned the lesson. It's like homework; you have to do the same kinds of problems until you get it right. Then you are ready to move to the next level. But we often stubbornly refuse to learn. It is not so much that we cannot learn; it is that we will not learn! We don't want to do it the way the teacher says. The Egyptians had ten plagues to get it right. As David later wrote:

> *Don't be like some senseless horse or mule,*
> > *whose movement must be controlled with a bit and a bridle.*
> *Don't be anything like that!*
> *The pain of the wicked is severe,*
> > *but faithful love surrounds the one who trusts the LORD.*
> > > (Psalm 32:9-10)

On one hand, you can imagine the sigh of relief collectively breathed out by the Israelites, to see the dead bodies of the Egyptians and their horses lying about on the shore, to see the powerful modern technology of war, the chariots, made useless, their wheels clogged with mud. On the other hand, as refugees of war and victims of disaster will testify, to see so many dead bodies at one time is traumatic, no matter whose they are. The sight of human beings who have been destroyed by wind, water, earthquake or war makes its impact on the mind and the spirit and alters one's perspective. The Israelites were already a traumatized people, having endured increasing levels of brutality during enslavement. At this point, they no doubt suffered some form of post-traumatic stress syndrome (PTS), which may have partially accounted for the many negative reactions they had for the next forty years. At the same time, they also experienced a collective change of mind toward Moses and toward God who was directing him.

> *Israel saw the amazing power of the LORD against the Egyptians. They were in awe of the LORD, and they believed in the LORD and in his servant Moses.* (Exodus 14:31)

They changed their minds about Moses and about God. They realized that the power of Egypt was nothing in comparison to the power of God. Human power must concede to God's power. When folk will not see the light, God has lightning, thunder, whirlwind, earthquake, and water at God's disposal. The wind and the waves obey God's will (Mark 4:41) even if human beings do not! The Israelites believed in God and they understood, perhaps for the first time, that Moses was God's representative on their behalf. Just hours before, they had declared that it would have been better for them to have stayed in Egypt (Exodus 14:11-12); but the outcome of this miraculous deed convinced them that Moses was working for their good on God's behalf. They changed their minds.

Discussion Questions
1. What has been the effect of natural disasters on your community?
2. If your community has not been affected, what can you do to help other communities which have experienced natural and/or human-made disasters like war and community violence?
3. Do you know someone who is suffering with Post Traumatic Stress Syndrome?

Then (Exodus 15:20-21)

What happens next is spontaneous rejoicing. The people had a praise break! As in any victory during ancient biblical times, the women come out with singing and dancing, playing instruments. Jephthah's daughter lost her life (Judges 11:30-35) because of this practice. Her father had pledged that if God would grant him a victory over the Amorites, he would sacrifice whatever greeted him upon his return home. When he came home, his daughter came out to greet him with tambourines and dancing. Blaming her, Jephthah grieved that he would have to give her as a burnt offering.

After David killed Goliath, the women came out dancing, playing tambourines and singing a short refrain that compared King Saul's accomplishments negatively to what David had done.

Saul has killed his thousands, but David has killed his tens of thousands!
David became the object of Saul's angry discontent (1 Samuel 18:6-9) because of this practice.

And even as Miriam's song is placed in verses 20-21 of chapter 15, the stories in the Bible are not always told in chronological order. Scholars* agree that Moses' song was inspired by Miriam's song even though it appears before her song in the record. One can imagine that upon a realization that God had scored this overwhelming victory, the women, led by Miriam, picked up their tambourines and began to dance and sing this short refrain over and over. This short refrain, a command for the people to praise God, tells the story of what happened in miniature. It commands the people to praise God and gives the reason why. Moses uses it to create a poem that illustrates God's relationship to the people of Israel.

For Discussion
Think of a time in your life when you suddenly broke out in praise to God. Share this experience with your classmates.

A Statement of Faith (Exodus 15:1-2)
The "Song of Moses" (Exodus 15:1-18) is considered to be "one of the oldest, most radical, and most important poems in the Old Testament,"* providing the primary, foundational theme of faith in God for the people of God. In utilizing Miriam's refrain, rather than addressing the people, commanding that they should praise God, Moses actually obeys the command. He and the entire congregation respond to Miriam's admonition to sing by actually singing, "I will sing . . . !" Our churches need to do this. Often we allow the soloist and choir to do all the praising and singing. They sing into microphones with instruments at top volume and we cannot hear our own voices, even if we try to sing. Miriam and her band of women were the praise team, the choir, and the soloist. Just as Moses and the rest of the Israelites joined in the celebration, this is what our churches and congregations should be doing today. Sing! Lift your voice in praise! It is not for the choir, praise team or soloists to do all of the singing. Their voices are not the only ones God wants to hear. As did Moses and the Israelites, let the people sing!

And what we sing is important. Songs express a statement of faith. Through song what we believe is embedded in our spirits. The hymn ascribed to Moses quickly shifts from a human focus to a focus on God. What folk are doing is always less important than who God is and what God has done. However, who God is and what God is doing is always grounded in how God desires and initiates relationship with humanity. Who is God? Moses declares: God is my strength; God is my power.
God is the joy and the strength of my life . . . God is my all in all.
(Robert J. Fryson)

TAKE A PRAISE BREAK, Celebrate the Works of God: Student

We have no strength and no power that does not come from the Lord.
> *The LORD is my strength and my shield. My heart trusts him. I was helped, my heart rejoiced, and I thank him with my song. The LORD is his people's strength; he is a fortress of protection for his anointed one.* (Psalm 28:7-8)

God is the one who rescues and saves! Moses proclaims: God has become my salvation! Moses identifies himself with God, the word "my" appearing five times in verse 2. He relates that this God, who delivered in the present time, is the same God associated with his ancestors. African American Gospel music is often criticized as having a me-ology rather than a theology. Those old songs tell of "my" circumstances and of what God has done for "me." Many claim a personal ownership of God: "Jesus is mine!" "Long as I got King Jesus!" "Oh, oh, oh, oh! What he's done for me!" Taking Moses' song as an example, it would seem that this tendency is in order. We should claim God as our own. We should recognize that it was God who delivered our ancestors. Too many people want to forget about American slavery and not talk about it. However, this is in direct opposition to the mandate of God. Those whose ancestors survived oppression should never forget, because it was God who rescued and delivered from that circumstance. We ought to know and tell about what God has done for all of the generations. It is a foundational American story. And whether black people were enslaved in the Caribbean or colonized in Africa, it is the same foundational story of human oppression versus God's power. When we remember, we can know what God is able to do in our present circumstance.

Discussion Questions
1. *Write down what you believe about God in five sentences or less.*
2. *What song best expresses a statement of faith for you?*

I Will Praise God for Freedom

Moses' song is a song of liberation. It continues (Exodus 15:3-18) by telling the story of what God had just done for the people. Its presence in the biblical record should remind us to always tell about the "right now" works of God. Our job is to tell about and promote what God is doing for the cause of liberation for people all over the world. Frederick Douglass said, "I prayed for twenty years but received no answer until I prayed with my [feet]." Just as Frederick Douglass used his feet and his legs to gain his liberation, just as during the Civil Rights Movement, people marched for freedom, a young girl named Phiona Mutesi used her feet to gain access to freedom, walking several miles each day to a mission site where she received a bowl of cereal and chess lessons. Before leaving the plantation, Douglass taught himself to read and to write. In today's world, literacy is critical to liberation. A very high percentage of persons currently incarcerated in the prison system of the United States are functionally illiterate. Now a teen world chess champion, Phiona Mutesi is learning to read. It has been found all across the world that women's access to literacy offers the best opportunity to uplift entire communities from the oppression of poverty and ignorance. It is God's desire that all should be free. As we speak out for justice, promote opportunities for education, and tell others about the works of God, let us praise God for freedom through Jesus Christ!

Discussion Questions
1. Why is it helpful to know about people like Phiona Mutesi?
2. What can you do to promote liberation in the world?

References
* Walter Brueggemann, ***The New Interpreter's Bible, Volume I***, (Nashville, TN: Abingdon Press), page 799, 1994.

LESSON 2

THE FAITH TO PRAY

ISAIAH 38:1-5, 19-21

Scripture
The prayer of the righteous is powerful and effective.
(James 5:16b, NRSV)

Opening Prayer
O God Who Sees and Hears,
Open my eyes to your wonders and my ears to your loving voice. Give me a powerful faith to pray in good times and bad, and give me a heart to share the story of your faithfulness. In Jesus' name. Amen.

Bible Lesson

1 At about that time Hezekiah became deathly sick. The prophet Isaiah, Amoz's son, came to him and said: "The LORD God says this: Put your affairs in order because you are about to die. You won't survive this." 2 Hezekiah turned his face to the wall and prayed to the LORD: 3 "Please, LORD, remember how I've done what you consider to be good." Then Hezekiah cried and cried. 4 Then the LORD's words came to Isaiah: 5 Go and say to Hezekiah: The LORD, the God of your ancestor David, says this: I have heard your prayer and have seen your tears. I will add fifteen years to your life. 9 A composition by Judah's King Hezekiah when he was sick and then recovered from his sickness:

19 The living, the living can thank you,
    as I do today.
      Parents will tell children
    about your faithfulness.
20 The LORD has truly saved me,
   and we will make music
    at the LORD's house
    all the days of our lives.
21 Then Isaiah said, "Prepare a salve made from figs, put it on the swelling, and he'll get better."

It's Time
During the time of American slavery, black people met in hush arbors and slave cabins to pray for freedom. After many years of a seeming "No" answer, God finally responded as with the Hebrew slaves upon the calling of Moses, setting the stage for the people to be brought into freedom.
> *"Then the LORD said, 'I've clearly seen my people oppressed in Egypt. I've heard their cry of injustice because of their masters. I know about their pain.'"* (Exodus 3:7)

Upon freedom, like the disciples in the new Christian movement in Acts 2:42, small bands of African Americans met in shacks and homes, praying and studying the Bible, then building church after church. Prayer meetings were an integral part of establishing black churches and in creating post slavery social change. Most of the direct action events carried out during the Civil Rights Movement started with prayer and purification. It could not have been easy to continue to pray to God in the midst of oppression and continued injustice. Nor is it easy to pray when any circumstance seems unyielding: difficult relationships, community violence, illness, money problems, career issues. Nevertheless, we are challenged to have enough faith to pray. As the father whose son was having fits told Jesus,
> *"I have faith; help my lack of faith!"* (Mark 9:24, CEB)
> *"I believe; help my unbelief!"* (NRSV)

As Jesus said, "This kind can come out only through prayer." (Mark 9:29, NRSV) We must ask God to increase our faith and give us the faith to pray.

The Back Story
Hezekiah was a good king. After years of royal and popular turning from God, 2 Chronicles, chapters 29-31 detail the many things he did to bring the people of Judah back into the worship of God. He re-sanctified the temple and reinstated the Levites and the priests, and re-established the all-important Passover celebration. He also took down the pagan places of worship and administered a system of worship and tithing to God throughout Judah. Hezekiah had a habit of prayer. He led the entire nation in prayer during times of national crisis.

As Mary McLeod Bethune (1875-1955), the daughter of former slaves, said in her Last Will and Testament, "Without faith nothing is possible, with it nothing is impossible." Faith in God is what gave a people with nothing the hope to build up families, churches and schools. After her hopes for becoming a missionary in Africa were thwarted, Bethune set her sights on establishing a school for the education of black girls in Daytona Beach, Florida. The story goes that she only had $1.50 at the time. Yet through the years, by connecting with benefactors like James Gamble of Proctor and Gamble, she built a school that remains today. Bethune-Cookman University is a United Methodist-affiliated, four-year, coed institution. She was not yet 30 when she began her quest in 1904.

Hezekiah had become king when he was 25 years old. He ruled for 29 years. However, right in the middle of his reign in an event described both in the Book of Isaiah and in 2 Kings 20:1-8, Hezekiah faced a situation that could have caused a crisis in faith.

Discussion Questions
1. What else do you know about Mary McLeod Bethune?
2. Why was Hezekiah considered to be a good king by biblical standards?
3. What are some situations that have caused you a crisis in faith?

Put Your Affairs in Order (Isaiah 38:1)

Do you have an executor, someone to take care of the business of your estate (however small or large) when you pass away?

Have you given power of attorney to a trustee, someone who will carry out your business affairs when you cannot?

Do you have an advance care plan that lets the doctors and hospital know your preferences concerning life-support, organ donation, the receiving of blood or nourishment?

Do you have a will that distributes your valuables among loved ones? How about an insurance policy that will take care of your funeral expenses and medical bills? Have you designated guardians for your children and teens in the event of your unexpected demise?

Is your paperwork in a place where the appointed people can get to them when needed?

Regardless of your age, it is time for you to start thinking about and taking care of these things. It is time for you to get your affairs in order!

Often people feel that dealing with end-of-life issues are indicators of a lack of faith. They act as though they are going to live forever, that God will not take them before their time, even though a tornado or car crash could! Despite the evidence and the admonition that no one knows the day or the hour (Matthew 24:36), many insist on being unprepared and leaving all of the gritty details and a hot mess for the people they love, to take care of after they die. Jesus' parable about the "Rich Fool" is a warning against greed, not against being prepared.

> *But God said to him, "Fool, tonight you will die. Now who will get the things you have prepared for yourself?"* (Luke 12:20)

Jesus encourages his disciples to stay awake, to be alert, and to be prepared for whatever comes!

> *Watch out! Stay alert! You don't know when the time is coming.*
> (Mark 13:33)

The prophet Isaiah had this word from the Lord for King Hezekiah, who had become ill. One thing was for sure; Hezekiah was dying. He was not going to get well. The prophet told him to get his affairs in order. This meant that he needed to manage his household in such a way that there would be an orderly transition of authority. Hezekiah needed to make sure that someone else knew the secrets of the kingdom, because he was not going to last long.

How difficult it must have been for Hezekiah to hear! It is always hard to hear that it is time to call a hospice service. However, most, who have had to utilize a hospice service, can testify to how helpful it is to know the stages of an inevitable death. Even as one can never be totally prepared for the death of a loved one, a hospice nurse can give palliative care, making sure that the dying is as comfortable as possible. Hospice personnel can help to interpret what is going on with the body and what actions on your part will be helpful to the patient. He or she can indicate that it is time to gather the family; far-flung relatives have just a few more days to say their goodbyes; it is time to call the pastor or chaplain.

Discussion Questions
1. *What do you need to do to get your affairs in order?*
2. *Have you ever been the executor or the person having to take care of a loved one's affairs when things were not in order? What was that like?*
3. *How does it feel to be the principal caregiver for someone who is dying?*

Hezekiah's Prayer (Isaiah 38:2-3)

Sickness and death are a part of life. While we do not always understand or agree, we can make sense of it when a life-long smoker comes up with lung cancer. But when someone, who has had healthy and righteous ways, exercised, eaten plenty of fruits and vegetables and avoided addictions (alcohol, tobacco, food, caffeine, drugs, sex), is diagnosed with an incurable disease, we are befuddled and angry. It's not fair! It is not helpful to be told that it is God's will. You don't want to hear it! And this was exactly Hezekiah's reaction. He turned his face to the wall, went into his secret closet and began to talk with God.

> *But when you pray, go to your room, shut the door, and pray to your Father who is present in that secret place. Your Father who sees what you do in secret will reward you.* (Matthew 6:6)

In looking at the text, one might not actually see the question. Yet, like Abraham when God had plans to destroy Sodom and Gommorah (Genesis 18:22-33), Hezekiah was pleading with God, begging God to change the situation. Like Job, Hezekiah was questioning God's judgment in allowing his situation. After all, "it is the living, who can thank God, not those who have gone down into death" (Isaiah 38:18-19). So often, it is heard in church that one should not question God, yet any close relationship should allow for questioning. God allows Job to ask questions and debate the fairness of his situation over and over. This is because of the intimate relationship that was between Job and God.

> *Oh, that I were as in the months of old, as in the days when God watched over me . . . When I was in my prime, when the friendship of God was upon my tent.* (Job 29:2 and 4, NRSV)

Hezekiah also had a close relationship with God, and in this dire time, he leaned upon that friendship, those past experiences, to plead his case. It was like going to a friend from whom you need something and reminding her, "Remember how I was there when such and such happened?" Or saying, "Hey Bro,' remember how I had your back when nobody else did?" And then you go on to say, "Well now, I need you to come through for me!" You cannot say these things to everyone you know; only to those who have stood in your corner when times were rough, only to those whom you believe will come through for you in the end, those in whom you have trust, those to whom you are able to let down your guard, show your vulnerabilities and insecurities, and open your heart. What better friend than God!

What a friend we have in Jesus, all our sins and griefs to bear!
What a privilege to carry, everything to God in prayer!

Hezekiah brought forward to God's mind all the things he had done to bring the people back to God, how God had counted these things as being good, how he had done them because they were the right things to do. Hezekiah pled his case. And then he cried.

For Discussion
Think about a time when you have poured out your heart to God over a difficult situation. How did you feel after that praying session?

God, Who Hears and Sees (Isaiah 38:4-5)

From the beginning of our faith history, God is recognized as one who hears and who sees. Both names, Ishmael and Samuel mean "God listens," "God hears" or "God has heard." Hagar, the Egyptian slave, was directed to name her son Ishmael, because during her pregnancy by Abraham, when Sarai mistreated her and she ran away into the wilderness, God heard her cry (Genesis 16:1-11). Hannah, who was mocked because she had not birthed any children, named her firstborn son Samuel because God heard her request when she poured out her heart in the temple at Shiloh (1 Samuel 1:1-19). All through the Book of Psalms, God is credited as one who listens.

I love the LORD because he hears my requests for mercy.
I'll call out to him as long as I live because he listens closely to me.
    (Psalm 116:1-2)

When Hezekiah turned his face to the wall and prayed, God heard him. When Hezekiah cried, God saw his tears. God responded immediately and sent the prophet Isaiah back to the king with a promise of healing and an additional fifteen years of life. God gave the response desired by Hezekiah and more. Often is the case, however, we may experience silence or a non-preferred result. Too often, others may drop on us the popular message, "It is already done!" leaving no room for an alternative response. Worse, if we do not get the asked for response from God, we may be encouraged to think that our faith is lacking or something is wrong with our prayer.

It might be better to operate from the perspective of the three Hebrew boys in the Book of Daniel, that whether God answers our prayers according to our desires or not, we will continue to serve the Lord.

> *"If our God—the one we serve—is able to rescue us from the furnace of flaming fire and from your power, Your Majesty, then let him rescue us. But if he doesn't, know this for certain, Your Majesty: we will never serve your gods or worship the gold statue you've set up."* (Daniel 3:17-18)

We must determine to serve God no matter the answer to the current problem, to build up our faith regardless of the outcome, to have the faith to continue to pray because communication with God strengthens us for whatever the journey may be.

Discussion Questions
1. How has prayer made the journey easier for you?
2. What are helpful ways to respond to people when they are experiencing trials and tribulations?

Hezekiah's Response (Isaiah 38:9; 19-21)

Hezekiah not only received word of God's response, he received a sign that his healing would happen (Isaiah 38:7-8), and a medication to effect the healing (verse 21). This is important. It may indicate that as in most serious illnesses, it would take a while for the healing to be completed. Therefore a sign was helpful in maintaining confidence in the prophecy. It is also important to note that God made use of the medical technology available. The prophet told Hezekiah's servants to prepare a salve (an ointment, a poultice) from figs and to put it on the swelling, (the boil, the infection) with a promise that Hezekiah would get better.

Part of Hezekiah's response would have been to take his medicine and to allow the servants to place the heated compress on his sore, which was probably very painful. Taking the medicine can be a struggle. How many parents have had to hold down children to get the medicine down their throats? How many patients neglect to follow new diets or take prescribed medications? How many refuse treatment that could help because the only sign they may have is the doctor's best judgment? All of us don't get a sign from God; we must trust that the best medical practice is being advised. We should read the pamphlets, get a second opinion, talk it out with knowledgeable people and pray. God has made the current medical technology available and it is a blessing when we can take advantage of it. God is the great physician who has charge of everything medical.

Hezekiah also responded with praise. The way the sentences are constructed, Hezekiah's praise break could have occurred either before he was healed (verse 22) or after he was healed (verse 9). What is clear is that he took a break to write a hymn of praise to God and he encouraged everyone to join him in praising God.

"We will make music at the LORD's house all the days of our lives."
(verse 20)

Hezekiah encourages the people to join him in praise so that the younger generations can know about God's faithfulness. It has been said that faith is caught rather than taught. This is no doubt true of a young man like Rev. Romal J. Tune. He would not have been taught faith from his drug-addicted mother, nor from the gang members who forced him to be a part when he was only eleven years old. Yet somehow at the age of sixteen, Tune managed to break way from the gang, moving all the way across country. He finished high school, entered the army and went to undergraduate school at Howard University. Somewhere along the way he heard about Jesus because he went to divinity school at Duke University, later founding Faith for Change, an organization that connects public schools with faith communities, empowering both to create safe spaces for at-risk children to learn and grow.* Faith for Change has multi-denominational partners across the United States. Because Tune's faith was caught, not taught, children benefit by having arenas in which they can develop into more complete human beings. If we keep praising God no matter the circumstances, young people will get the message that anytime is the right time for a praise break, Hallelujah!

Discussion Questions
1. *How can your church partner with the schools in its neighborhood to provide spiritual and academic flourishing for children and teens?*
2. *Choose someone in the class to go online at http://faithforchange.org/ to learn more about Faith for Change.*

Reference
*http://www.huffingtonpost.com/2012/03/30/faith-inspires-faith-for-change-graduation-ministry_n_1392022.html

LESSON 3

THE SAVIOR'S BIRTH

Scripture Luke 2:8-15

"Your Savior is born today in David's city. He is Christ the Lord."

(Luke 2:11)

Opening Prayer

God of Revelation,
Shine your light and your glory upon me that I may hear a new message from you. Take away my fear of the unexpected and the new and let me be a messenger of hope for what you are doing right now! In Jesus' name. Amen.

Bible Lesson

8 Nearby shepherds were living in the fields, guarding their sheep at night. 9 The Lord's angel stood before them, the Lord's glory shone around them, and they were terrified. 10 The angel said, "Don't be afraid! Look! I bring good news to you – wonderful, joyous news for all people. 11 Your Savior is born today in David's city. He is Christ the Lord. 12 This is a sign for you: you will find a newborn baby wrapped snugly and lying in a manger." 13 Suddenly a great assembly of heavenly forces was with the angel praising God. They said, 14 "Glory to God in heaven, and on earth peace among those whom he favors." 15 When the angels returned to heaven, the shepherds said to each other, "Let's go right now to Bethlehem and see what's happened. Let's confirm what the Lord has revealed to us."

TAKE A PRAISE BREAK, Celebrate the Works of God: Student

It's Time

In the Hebrew, "Bethlehem" means "house of bread." How suitable that the one whom we call "The Bread of Life" was born there! Bethlehem was the ancestral home of King David and it is from his genealogical line that the one anointed by God to bring salvation was to come (Micah 5:1-5). David, himself, was a shepherd boy as the old Negro Spiritual testifies.

> *Little David was a shepherd boy.*
> *He killed Goliath and shouted for joy.*
> *Little David, play on your harp, Hallelu! Hallelu!*

As the youngest and the least in a family of boys, David was tending the sheep when Samuel came looking for someone to replace Saul as the king of Israel (1 Samuel 16:1-13). Again, how fitting that the first people to hear the news about the Savior's birth were shepherds! Rather than writing the vision, the angels verbally testified concerning the appointed time (Habakkuk 2:2-3). In song, they heralded the birth of Jesus Christ. And it all happened in and around the village of Bethlehem.

The Back Story

It is often assumed that everybody knows the story of Jesus' birth. After all, Christmas decorations sometimes go up before Halloween and certainly before Thanksgiving Day. The stores must be ready for Black Friday, one of the few days and ways in which "black" is used positively. Black Friday is the day when many shoppers begin their quest for Christmas presents. If the shopping is good, business owners breathe a sigh of relief. They can remain open for another year. They are "in the black" with balanced budgets and good profits. As people search the malls for the best buys, visiting Santa Claus, listening to sleigh bells and viewing elaborate decorations, there are those who have no idea that all of the hoopla starts with Jesus Christ.

They do not know about the Virgin Mary, a teenaged mother, or about her husband, Joseph's leap of faith in standing by her. They discount the power of a Roman government that caused them to travel to Bethlehem or the rigors of traveling by mule. They may not identify with shepherds or believe in heavenly messengers. For them good news is low prices, not incarnation: a Holy Spirit pregnancy, a brand-new star-child being born in a barn, God coming in the flesh to be among the people, Immanuel. That God identifies with those for whom there is no room, with folk who must flee injustice, as told by Ida B. Wells-Barnett (1862-1931) is not news they want to hear. That the least of these are the first on God's list is not their concern. They just don't know. They may not care. Christmas, after all, is about shopping!

Shepherds (Luke 2:8)

Shepherds are featured prominently in biblical literature. From Abel, a keeper of sheep (Genesis 4:2) to Psalm 23 to Jesus, the Good Shepherd (John 10:11), the skill and art of shepherding extends from leading animals to leading people. It is the job of shepherds to keep the flock safe, to be with them and calm their fears, to get to know them and to make sure their needs are met. In Ezekiel 34, God holds the leaders of Israel accountable for doing the exact opposite.

> *Thus says the LORD God: Ah, you shepherds of Israel who have been feeding yourselves! Should not shepherds feed the sheep? You eat the fat, you clothe yourselves with the wool, you slaughter the fatlings; but you do not feed the sheep. You have not strengthened the weak, you have not healed the sick, you have not bound up the injured, you have not brought back the strayed, you have not sought the lost, but with force and harshness you have ruled them.*
> (Ezekiel 34:2b-4, NRSV)

Here, we see what is expected of shepherds, which is why in Luke we find them living with their animals. Jesus said that sheep know the voice of their shepherd. They know his voice and he knows each by name.

> *The one who enters through the gate is the shepherd of the sheep. The guard at the gate opens the gate for him, and the sheep listen to his voice. He calls his own sheep by name and leads them out.* (John 10:2-4)

The shepherds in Luke were in the mountainous area of Judea, currently called the West Bank, where both agriculture and sheep farming have been practiced for ages. In the winter, the sheep graze in the lowlands, with shepherds moving them to the hilltops for summer grazing. *The Messiah* by George Frederic Handel is a musical work with choir, soloists and orchestra. It tells the story of Jesus' birth, death and resurrection. This passage, "There were shepherds, abiding the fields, keeping watch over their flocks by night (KJV)," sung by an angelic soprano voice, is introduced by a section entitled "Pastoral Symphony." The string section (violins, violas, cellos) plays a calm lullaby to create the environment in which all is as it should be at night, all creatures at rest, shepherds and sheep alike drowsing, sleeping, and dreaming. And suddenly this peaceful scene is interrupted by the presence of an angel.

For Discussion
What are some of the qualities of a good leader?

Angels (Luke 2:9)

Angels are also featured prominently in biblical literature. The appearance of one represents the very appearance of God, often used interchangeably with God. In Genesis, while the text describes Jacob as struggling with a man (Genesis 32:24), Jacob recognizes that it is God with whom he was wrestling. Jacob does not let go of the man until he receives a blessing.

> Your name won't be Jacob any longer, but Israel, because you struggled with God and men and won. (Genesis 33:28)

Jacob named the place Peniel, meaning "face of God" because he had seen God face-to-face and lived.

Angels are messengers of God. From Samson's mother (Judges 13:1-7) to John's father, Zechariah (Luke 1:5-20) to Mary, the mother of Jesus (Luke 1:26-38), angels have announced the coming of children that are critical to the salvation history of God's people. The angel told Zechariah:

> I am Gabriel. I stand in God's presence. I was sent to speak to you and to bring this good news to you. Know this: what I have spoken will come true at the proper time. (Luke 1:19-20a)

The angel represented the mighty God. Zechariah had graciously received a message of good news directly from God. Rather than be appropriately star-struck, Zechariah, a priest, chose to go on his own understanding. The shepherds, however, were awed and terrified at the angel's presence with God's glorious light. Perhaps, it was because they were shepherds.

> Trust in the LORD with all your heart; don't rely on your own intelligence. (Proverbs 3:5)

If God shows up in the ordinary affairs of our lives what will be our response? Zechariah was used to handling the holy things of God. For years he had taken his turn in the temple at Jerusalem. While the angel had startled him, his fear had not overcome his sense of reason. In the conversation about he and Elizabeth having a baby, he immediately went to the natural, the fact that they were old, forgetting that God decides what is natural and what is not. At any time, Creator God can supersede what human beings know as natural. The shepherds were afraid, yet as students of nature, as men of a different social status, who may have realized that they did not know everything, perhaps their hearts and minds were more open to what God would reveal.

For Discussion

When have you experienced a time when God showed up in the ordinary?

The Message (Luke 2:10-14)

The angel had a message from God. After calming the shepherds' fears, he shared it. The news that a Savior was born in David's city was intended as good news for all people for all time: from the priest to the pauper, from the shepherd to the shopper, from then till now. That Jesus Christ (Messiah, Anointed One) is Lord is a message that should bring joy to every nation and people. How is that? Here is a child whose parents were so unprepared that the mother ends up giving birth among the animals in a stranger's barn. They had not had a chance to go shopping for the newest baby equipment. No one threw her a baby shower. (Should unmarried teens be given one?) An animal trough and rags had to do. Here is a child with parents so poor that when they brought him to the temple (Luke 2:21-24), they had to offer pigeons (Leviticus 12:8). The reality is that in the 21st century, 80 percent of the world's population is still very poor, living on less than $1.25 a day. According to UNICEF, almost 22,000 children die each day due to poverty. "They die quietly in some of the poorest villages in the world, far removed from the scrutiny and conscience of the world."* This child, the Anointed One, grew up to announce that his purpose in the world was:

> *"To preach good news to the poor, to proclaim release to the prisoners and recovery of sight to the blind, to liberate the oppressed, and to proclaim the year of the Lord's favor."* (Luke 4:18-19)

The angel had an inclusive message of good news about the ultimate bearer of good news for all people!

Suddenly, a great assembly of the heavenly forces, multiple angels and perhaps other entities (2 Kings 6:16-17), backed up the singular angel's announcement with singing. That God should choose to interrupt the natural flow of things was a heavenly revolution intended to lead to an earthly revolution that the first shall be last and the last shall be first. But the shepherds did not know this. They did know that God had sought them out with an amazing revelation. They did know that something wonderful was happening right before their eyes, a praise break in the sky! They heard a message of *shalom*, a promise of wholeness for all people, including them. And that is good news that should bring joy to the world.

Discussion Questions
1. What is your experience with poverty?
2. What would the first being last and the last being first look like in your community?

An Appropriate Response (Luke 2:15)
When the glorious vision was gone, the shepherds struck up a conversation.
 "Did you see that?"
 "Did you hear what I heard?"
 "Those were angels, right?"
 "Must be God!"
 "It's time to go!"
 "Well then, let's go!"
 "Bethlehem, right?"
 "That little town right over the hill!"
 "I wanna see what those angels were talkin' about!"

The shepherds had an appropriate response. They went to check things out. The shepherds not only went to Bethlehem to see for themselves, once they saw Jesus with his parents, they told others about it and they had their own praise break (verses 16-20). An appropriate response to the good news of Jesus Christ is to tell someone else. It was news that impacted the shepherds in a positive way and they wanted to share it.

Sometimes, however, there is news that can impact communities negatively, but for the common good, the news must still be shared. Such is the case with Ida B. Wells-Barnett and Dr. Erica Warner. As one of the founders of the NAACP, Wells-Barnett was an investigative journalist during the time when segregation became firmly entrenched in American society. Living in Memphis, she discovered the facts about lynchings and injustices and exposed them in her writings, such as *Southern Horrors in All Its Phases* and *The Red Record* (1892-1894). She believed that it was an appropriate response for black people to leave the South and go where they would be treated more fairly. Many took her up on this. And indeed, she also had to relocate to Chicago, Illinois for her own safety. Wells-Barnett was an advocate for women's rights and an orator who believed "The way to right wrongs is to turn the light of truth upon them."

Erica Warner also spreads news that includes hard truths. She is a medical researcher at Harvard who wants to shed light on the risk factors that cause black women to die more frequently of breast cancer than any other group. Her studies showed that black women are 50 percent more likely to die within the first three years of being diagnosed and that body size and obesity negatively affect the occurence and outcomes. Additionally, black women tend to discover their cancers at a later stage, with too many not having easy access to medical care. Her research was presented in 2012 at the Conference on The Science of Cancer Health Disparities. With a black woman shedding light on this truth, the community has a chance to have an appropriate response. Individuals may choose to make some lifestyle changes in order to decrease risk.

> *"You are truly my disciples if you remain faithful to my teaching. Then you will know the truth, and the truth will set you free."*
> (John 8:31b-32)

What is our response to truth-telling? The truth sets us free but first we have to know the truth. Those who know the truth must spread the news and share it. We must be willing to be like Ida B. Wells-Barnett and uncover injustice and tell about it. Like the shepherds we must be willing to adjust our behavior and respond to the news, whether news about health disparities in the black community or news about the teachings of Jesus Christ. Jesus came to bring peace to the world; peace that is not just an absence of conflict, but wholeness, freedom from fear, experiencing health and abundant life. Jesus is the way, the truth and the life. We must not only tell about it, we must work toward it and live it out. Get up and go, like the shepherds did!

Discussion Questions

1. How is your church involved with peace and justice ministries?
2. What can churches do to lead people to better health practices?
3. When is the last time you told someone about the good news of Jesus Christ?

References
* http://www.globalissues.org/article/26/poverty-facts-and-stats#src4

LESSON 4

LOST AND FOUND

Luke 15:8-10

Scripture
"The God of heaven will give us success!" (Nehemiah 2:20a)

Opening Prayer
O God of Amazing Grace,
Give me the right attitude as I reach out to those who may be misplaced but are searching for you in this experience. Let me know the joy of celebrating with all of heaven for those who come, seeking success in Christ. In Jesus' name. Amen.

Bible Lesson
8 "Or what woman, if she owns ten silver coins and loses one of them, won't light a lamp and sweep the house, searching her home carefully until she finds it? 9 When she finds it, she calls together her friends and neighbors, saying, 'Celebrate with me because I've found my lost coin.' 10 In the same way, I tell you, joy breaks out in the presence of God's angels over one sinner who changes both heart and life."

It's Time

One of the most universally liked songs in the world is "Amazing Grace" by John Newton; the first verse is the one everyone knows.

> Amazing grace, how sweet the sound: that saved a wretch like me.
> I once was lost but now am found, was blind but now I see.

It may have been a while since you as an adult have been physically lost. Those adults experiencing the first stages of Alzheimer's disease may know the feeling of 'lostness' all too well. But practically all adults have experienced episodes of misplacing something from time to time, those pesky keys, for example, without which we can do nothing. What a relief when we find that item which has been lost! What a blessing to know that in our spiritual lostness, God diligently searches for us! To transition from a state of being lost or losing something to a state of sanctuary is an occasion for celebration.

The Back Story (Luke 15:1-7, 11-32)

Jesus was a master storyteller. The art of storytelling is a teaching method that opens the mind to new possibilities. Sometimes rather than beating another person over the head with facts, a story may open ears and part the clouds of judgment. Jesus was teaching to a group that included tax collectors and sinners. The religious experts were complaining about it. Using money, an animal and a human being as object lessons, Jesus responds by telling three stories about what makes God and heaven happy. He tells a story about a shepherd who looks for one lost sheep out of ninety-nine and how he calls other shepherds to celebrate with him when he finds the lost sheep. He also tells a story about a young man who demands his portion of his father's wealth, blows it all, and has to come home. The father throws a "welcome home" party for his son.

In between these two stories, he talks about a woman who has lost one of ten silver coins. The coins could represent a poor woman's dowry, which would have been worn as a necklace or they could represent her wages or household savings. The coins would have been denarii, one of which was paid to a man for a day's labor (Matthew 20:1-2). A woman was paid half of that for a day's labor. Women in ancient Palestine worked in the fields (Ruth 2:1-9) to help keep the household.

A story with a woman as the principle character, no matter how short, was no doubt very shocking to his listeners. In a society concerned with purity, women were considered the most unclean of all! Even today, among

Orthodox Jews, it is forbidden for a man to touch a woman because he can never know if she is bleeding. This is based on purity laws in the Book of Leviticus, chapter 12. He cannot touch even anything she has touched or he is rendered unclean. Jesus uses a woman as the main character because it was his mission to seek the lost and the least, and in ancient society only a child was considered to be less than a woman. One could say that this is still true, considering the fact that even in America, women are paid 70 percent of what a man earns for doing the same job.

For Discussion
Considering the fact that many households in the black community are headed by women, what effect might a lack of equal pay for equal work have on the black community as a whole?

A Teaching Moment (Luke 15:8-10)

The kind of story that Jesus was using is called parable. A parable is a brief narrative that acts as an illustration of a universal, spiritual, or some would say, heavenly truth or concept. In addition to parable, Jesus also uses a rhetorical device of questioning to encourage his critics to think, possibly persuading his hearers to another way of thinking, not necessarily expecting an oral answer but a new perspective. He asks his audience to consider the plight of a woman who has lost one of her ten silver coins and lights a lamp, using precious oil, and sweeps every inch of her house, using precious time and energy, in her search for the lost coin. When she finds it, she calls together all of her friends and neighbors, compelling them to celebrate with her the recovery of her coin. Jesus then makes a comparison. His point was to help his critics to understand why he welcomes and eats with sinners (Luke 15:1-2). Jesus says that there is also a party in heaven when one sinner changes heart and mind.

For Discussion
What is your favorite parable? What did you learn from it?

God, Who Searches

These stories not only illustrate what happens in heaven when that which is lost has been found, they also demonstrate the nature of the one who searches-- God, who is always initiating contact with human beings, all of whom are prone to do the opposite of what God wants. Psalm 139 gives a detailed directory of how we cannot escape the interest of God, with verse one saying,

> *O LORD, you have searched me and known me.* (NRSV)
> *LORD, you have examined me. You know me.* (CEB)

Verses 7-10 indicate the impossibility of getting away from God; whether to the height or the depths, in the night or at dawn, God sees us and knows where we are.

God comes to where we are. Even after Adam and Eve directly disobeyed God by eating the fruit of the tree of the knowledge of good and evil, desiring to be like God, it is God who searched them out (Genesis 2:17; 3:10). They tried to hide but God initiated contact, calling out to Adam, asking, "Where are you?" God went looking for Hagar in the wilderness. The angel of the Lord found her and called her by name, asking, "Where did you come from and where are you going?" (Genesis 16:8). When Samuel was just a small boy God called out to him in the temple as many times as it took, until he was able to understand what was going on (1 Samuel 3:1-10).

When Jonah tried to run from the responsibility God had given him (Jonah 1:17), God sought him out and brought him back by means of a storm and a large fish. And when the righteous Pharisee Saul "was still spewing out murderous threats against the Lord's disciples" (Acts 9:1), Jesus met him on the road to Damascus, asking,

> "*Saul, why are you harassing me?*"
> *Saul asked, "Who are you, Lord?"*
> "*I am Jesus, whom you are harassing.*" (Acts 9:4b-5)

Even when we do not know who God is, God knows each one and desires communion with us all. The woman in Jesus' story was not content with nine of ten coins. Nor is God content until all come to Christ. God calls us again and again. Like the woman lighting a lamp, God sent Jesus Christ, the Light of the World to show us the way. God sifts us and tries us like the woman with her broom.

> *This is right and it pleases God our Savior, who wants all people to be saved and to come to a knowledge of the truth.* (1 Timothy 2:3-4)

> *The Lord isn't slow to keep his promise, as some think of slowness, but he is patient toward you, not wanting anyone to perish but all to change their hearts and lives.* (2 Peter 3:9)

A woman's paltry coin may have seemed beneath the interest of scribes and Pharisees, who were people of comparative means and position in that society. However, Jesus told this story for them to see that there is no one who is not worthy of God's interest, even a woman with meager means. Those who are the least in human society rank high on God's list. All of heaven not only take notice but indeed celebrate big time when the lost and the least are found and enter into sanctuary with God.

For Discussion
Have you ever experienced God's seeking of you? What was that like?

Negro Pennies

Back in the day of American society, the meager resources allowed to black Americans were not always welcomed in established banks. During the days when segregation was being solidified, the owners of white banks were afraid that black customers would drive away their white depositors. While some believe that all money is green and therefore speaks for itself, in this case, Negro pennies were not worth it.

Maggie Lena Walker of Richmond, Virginia had been working with the Independent Order of St. Luke since she was fourteen years old. She had almost single-handedly revived this mutual aid society that specialized in making sure black people had enough money to bury themselves and to aid one another in sickness. In 1901, at its annual convention, Walker laid out a plan to start a savings bank for Blacks. "First, we need a savings bank. Let us put our moneys together; let us use our moneys; let us put our money at usury among ourselves, and reap the benefit ourselves. Let us have a bank that will take the nickels and turn them into dollars." She argued why should black people "feed the lion of [racial] prejudice" by patronizing white banks?*

On July 28, 1903, when the charter for the St. Luke Penny Savings Bank was issued by Virginia's Corporation Commission, Maggie Lena Walker became the first woman of any race to charter and/or become president of a bank. The bank opened its doors on November 3, 1903. Accounts were started with as little as $0.31. Walker encouraged families and children to open bank accounts, setting up a program that allowed children to open an account when they had saved up 100 pennies. Walker's stewardship and vision for this bank enabled it to survive the Great Depression. As other banks, especially black-owned banks, began to close, in the late 1920's Walker took action to have St Luke's merge with two other black-owned banks. Using St. Luke's building, and with Walker becoming the Chairman of the Board of Directors until her death (1934), the Consolidated Bank and Trust (est. 1930) lasted into the 21st century. The year 2009 ended its run as the oldest continuously black-owned bank in America (see note, page 33.) It provided employment, helped African Americans realize home ownership goals, was a source of pride to the community, and demonstrated Maggie Lena Walker's belief that "If a solution is not enduring, it's not really a solution."

For Discussion
Do you patronize black businesses? Why or why not?

Keep on Dreaming

While the economic dreams of too many African Americans are hampered by a lack of wealth and opportunity, Walker's story is inspirational as to what can be done with very little--pennies and nickels. Black people in larger numbers certainly have more resources available in 2014 than in 1904. Her "bank serves as a reminder of the lasting and beneficial impact one woman's dream and perseverance can have on an entire community."*

Good stewardship of what we have is one of the keys to success. Since 1970, *Black Enterprise*, "the premier business, investing and wealth-building resource for African Americans, has provided essential business information and advice to professionals, corporate executives, entrepreneurs and decision makers."** Earl G. Graves, Jr. not only fulfilled his dream of becoming a professional basketball player (Philadelphia 76'ers, Milwaukee Bucks, and the Cleveland Cavaliers), he is now the president and CEO (Chief Executive Officer) of this enterprise started as a magazine by his father, forty years ago. After earning a Master's of Business Admnistration from Harvard and gaining experience at Morgan Stanley, Graves joined the staff in 1988. He has added other communications strategies in order to reach as many people as possible. Through its "Wealth for Life" component, the organization seeks to educate and empower its audience to become full participants in the global economy.

The economic downturn of 2008 hit the black community hard. There were many housing foreclosures and job losses among African Americans. A proverb in the black community is: "When white folks get a cold, black folks get pneumonia!" While many of the loans approved in the unremitting greed of the financial institutions should never have been, even the most prepared of African American young people became once again the last hired when things began to turn around. Nevertheless, we must encourage all people, especially young people, to exhibit the persistence of Maggie Lena Walker and of the woman in Jesus' story, being relentless in our quest for success and using every tool available.

> *Let's not get tired of doing good, because in time we'll have a harvest if we don't give up. So then, let's work for the good of all whenever we have an opportunity, and especially for those in the household of faith.* (Galatians 6:9-10)

God, who values us all, will give us success as we practice good stewardship of our earthly treasure to the best of our abilities. God desires for us to be good stewards of every good gift. We've got to keep on dreaming, realizing that Jesus had the ultimate "prosperity gospel," that we lay up treasure in heaven, first desiring God's kingdom and righteousness, putting our first loyalty to the value system of Jesus Christ.

> *I came so that they could have life—indeed, so that they could live life to the fullest.* (John 10:10b)

> *Where your treasure is, there your heart will be also.* (Matthew 6:21)

When we lay our treasure in the refuge of God's sanctifying grace, all of heaven celebrates. When we see others choosing abundant life in Christ, we should take a praise break. Hallelujah!

Discussion Questions

1. Good financial stewardship for Christians is often defined as paying a tithe (one-tenth of earnings), saving a tenth and living on the rest. How does this work for you?
2. What other aspects of our lives besides money should be included in a stewardship plan?

References
* http://www.nps.gov/mawa/the-st-luke-penny-savings-bank.htm
** http://www.blackenterprise.com/about-us/

Note
As of 2013, Citizens Savings Bank and Trust Co. (Citizens Bank) of Nashville, Tennessee, was the oldest, continuously operating, minority-owned bank in the United States. It was founded by R.H. Boyd, Preston Tylor and J.C. Napier in 1904, a few months after Maggie Lena Walker's St. Luke Penny Savings Bank.

LESSON 5

MARCHING TO ZION

Mark 11:7-9; Luke 19:39-40

Scripture
"Hosanna! Blessings on the one who comes in the name of the Lord!"
(Mark 11:9b)

Opening Prayer
Blessed Jesus,
We praise you, for you have brought us through many troubles and trials. Thank you for the leaders you have sent us. Let us continue to work for the coming of your peaceable kingdom, in your name we pray. Amen.

Bible Lesson
Mark 11:7-9
7 They brought the colt to Jesus and threw their clothes upon it, and he sat on it. 8 Many people spread out their clothes on the road while others spread branches cut from the fields. 9 Those in front of him and those following were shouting, "Hosanna! Blessings on the one who comes in the name of the Lord!

Luke 19:39-40
39 Some of the Pharisees from the crowd said to Jesus, "Teacher, scold your disciples! Tell them to stop! 40 He answered, "I tell you, if they were silent, the stones would shout."

It's Time
2013 marked the 150th anniversary of the signing of the Emancipation Proclamation and the 50th anniversary of the March on Washington for Jobs and Freedom. Just as the disciples of Jesus took to the streets to welcome to Jerusalem someone they thought would bring more justice and peace to their lives, in 1963 Washington, D.C. hosted people of all backgrounds marching for economic parity. They came by train, bus, car and plane to demonstrate in hopes of calling attention to the need for jobs and justice. There are those who remember, who were there and who benefitted from the landmark legislation and affirmative action practices that gave African Americans a more level playing ground in American life. The March in August 1963 was a springboard for freedom movements all over the world, from women's and migrant workers', to the independence of African nations from colonialism, to strengthening the will of black South Africans to fight against apartheid. One of the fruits of that movement was the election of Barack Obama, the first African American to serve as the President of the United States, forty-five years later. Another outcome was renewed terrorism against black Americans as demonstrated by the bombing of the Sixteenth Avenue Baptist Church (September 15, 1963) in Birmingham, Alabama, resulting in the death of four young girls. Renewed terrorism continues to be demonstrated in the fact that President Obama has received more death threats than any other president in the history of the United States.

Despite these negative reactions to the cry for justice, people of faith must keep on walking and talking for and with Jesus, helping the world to understand his mission as uttered when he began his ministry:
> *"The Spirit of the Lord is upon me because the Lord has anointed me to preach good news to the poor, to proclaim release to the prisoners and recovery of sight to the blind, to liberate the oppressed, and to proclaim the year of the Lord's favor."* (Luke 4:18-19)

The Back Story
Because it was near the season of Passover, Jesus and the disciples were on their way to Jerusalem, where he knew that he would be mistreated and killed. Just outside Jerusalem, as they neared the villages of Bethany and Bethphage on the Mount of Olives, Jesus instructed his disciples to go into the village and find a colt that had never been ridden. He told them that if someone questioned why they were untying the animal to tell them that the master needed it. The disciples found the colt.

Jesus' procession on Palm Sunday reflected the coronation traditions of the Hebrew people. When King David got old, in keeping with his promise to Bathsheba, he made sure that Solomon was made the king of Israel. Accompanied by a crowd crying, "Long live King Solomon," Solomon rode on his father's mule. He was then anointed by a priest and a prophet, and the trumpet was blown as people shouted with joy (1 Kings 1:28-40). When Jehu was made king, a prophet anointed him with oil, the trumpet was blown, and the people took their cloaks and spread them on the bare steps (2 Kings 9:4-13). Psalm 118:25-26, which the people were shouting, also gives an instruction to "bind the festal procession with branches"(v. 27b, NRSV). The ancient procession was a parade to the capital city, where the people gathered to crown their king, "Wonderful Counselor, Mighty God, Eternal Father, Prince of Peace," on whose shoulders would rest the authority of the government (Isaiah 9:6).

Save Us! (Mark 11:7-9)

Jesus' disciples were obedient and delivered the colt to him. They threw their clothes on the animal and he sat on it. As the parade began some people laid their clothing on the ground in front of Jesus. Some people cut branches from the fields and spread them along the pathway to Jerusalem. People were in front of him and behind him, shouting the ancient greeting, "Hosanna! Blessings on the one who comes in the name of the Lord!" They welcomed the one who for them represented a return of the kingdom of Israel as ruled by David, who established the nation of Israel as a force to be reckoned with and made its capital, Jerusalem.

It is interesting to note that the word "Hosanna!" was a traditional greeting for a king, meaning "Save us!" It indicated the expectations of the people for what a king would do, save them from oppression, from poverty, from enemies, from whatever might be wrong in the national life at the time. At the same time, Jesus' name means "God is salvation." The name, Jesus, is the Greek form of the Hebrew/Aramaic name Yeshua/Yehoshua or Joshua, all of which mean, "God is salvation." So the people are crying out for Jesus, "God is salvation" to save them. Christians believe that Jesus is God. And so the people shouting, "Save us! Save us to the nth degree!" (Hosanna in the highest!), takes on a meaning that is more than political. Jesus is God who saves us in ways the people at that time could not even imagine. That "the nth degree" was for eternity was not in their minds. They wanted some relief from oppression and poverty right now! This is why they so quickly turned on him when it became apparent that he would not lead a revolution and dethrone Herod. What good was he for, anyway, and why had they risked their necks to make a parade for a royal imposter?

For Discussion
People are constantly disappointed by those in leadership positions. Indian Leader Mahatma Ghandi said, "Be the change you wish to see in the world." How can you apply this to your life?

Risky Business (Luke 19:39)

Just as there were FBI agents at every meeting of the Civil Rights Movement, one who was a trusted and prolific photographer (Ernest Withers*); just as persons faithful to the goals of the movement asked John Lewis to change his speech for the Washington March because it was deemed too radical; Jesus and his followers had to contend with people who were either spies or those who felt they had the best interest of the people at heart over and above what Jesus was doing. Jesus needed to tone it down! It's risky to be in a movement, to be part of a crowd that is moving toward the capital city, advocating for change. It is better to keep your mouth shut and your head down!

Something that is often not understood is that in first century Palestine, the Jewish people as an identifiable group were in a fight for their political and cultural life. Their culture had been watered down and influenced by Greek culture for generations. Politically, they had been exiled, returned to the land as vassals for a foreign entity and finally conquered and colonized by the Romans. People of color in recent centuries have experienced all of this. Liberia, for example, was a colony of the United States, a place to send newly freed slaves, who would act as agents for the United States in keeping indigenous groups under control and as an export funnel for the rich resources of iron and rubber. What was the culture of these newly freed people? Did they know or appreciate the culture or political structure of the people who were already living on the coast of Africa? Just as in ancient Israel, this kind of agenda created generations of turmoil and discontent.

In any suppressed community, there are factions that believe "you've got to go along to get along." They are the ones who have a stake in things the way they are. They have a safe job and access, though limited, to the people in power. They don't want to make any waves; they are afraid that they will lose what they have. As quiet as it is kept, there were many black people that fit into this category during the Civil Rights Movement. They just wished that the marchers would stop all that rabble rousing. They believed in gradual progress and being accommodating. After all, they had made it, hadn't they? In the Jewish community, the Sadducees would fit this category. They had an agreement with the Roman government concerning the temple tax. They were even allowed to have their own coinage, a lucrative set-up for this class.

And then there were the Pharisees, a scholastic and legalistic class. In a Roman/Hellenistic world in which all things Jewish were different and therefore negative, they were trying to stem the tide of assimilation. What does it mean to be Jewish? How do we apply the laws of Moses in our modern setting? During the 1960's and 70's, Blacks in America went from being colored, to Negro, to Black to African American. They went from despising nappy hair to sporting Afro hairstyles and braids, from hating African heritage to wanting to learn more. This is what the Pharisees were about: identity. Following the laws of Moses is what set them apart as a people. It is one of the reasons they had so many questions for Jesus. His teaching was clearly authoritative. They were trying to figure out if he was one of them or not. Or was he a Zealot?

Ah, the Zealots! They wanted to defend the ancient kingdom of Israel by any means necessary. Like the rhetoric of the Black Panthers and others, their speech and activity were radical and fiery. In a few decades, such radical talk and activity would bring on the full power of the Roman Empire against this tiny region, crushing it. The Roman government would decide not to tolerate these different Jews any more and dispersed them so permanently, that most Jews all over the world could only **imagine** going to Jerusalem for Passover, which is how Palm Sunday began, until after World War II.

No wonder the religious leaders became alarmed when the people started treating Jesus as the coming king! To hold an inauguration parade for a king other than the one seated by the Roman government could be considered acts of sedition and treason, which was ultimately the crimes for which Jesus was crucified.

For Discussion
For Rome, Jesus was a political prisoner. What were his crimes according to the Jewish court?

Silence is Betrayal (Luke 19:40)

It has always been risky to speak out against injustice, even in the United States. Both Paul Robeson and Adam Clayton Powell paid a heavy price in terms of their careers for doing so. Paul Robeson was banned from the United States and Powell lost his chairmanship in the House of Representatives. Of course, Martin Luther King, Jr. paid with his life, partly because he refused to merely be prophetic concerning "black" issues but insisted on being a full human being. On April 4, 1967, in a sermon at the Riverside Church in New York City, King began to speak out against the injustice of the Vietnam War. He was assassinated exactly one year later.

In this sermon, King affirmed that he was in solidarity with the organization, Clergy and Laymen Concerned about Vietnam, which had recently put forth that "silence is betrayal." With this sermon, he alienated President Johnson who had been instrumental in the passage of civil rights legislation, and many others, both political and religious, black and white, who felt that King should "stay in his lane!" King believed that his lane was inclusive of all poor people, even the Vietnamese peasant, that nonviolence was not only for black Americans, but for the United States government. He pointed out the injustice of sending black soldiers who did not have freedom and could not get a job in America to fight a war supporting the ideals of freedom, democracy and capitalism. He defended his receipt of the Nobel Peace Prize as a commission to work toward the unity of all people and that his opposition to war was deeply rooted in his commitment to the Gospel of Jesus Christ. He compared the testing of newly developed weapons of war on the Vietnamese peasants to the activities of Germany's Third Reich. He called on the United States to stop the bombing, that the choice was between "nonviolent coexistence" and "violent co-annihilation." Dr. King called for America to not only take on the ethics of the Good Samaritan but also to transform the Jericho Road so that people do not keep getting beaten up by life's journey!**

Silence is betrayal! This is basically what Jesus told the Pharisees who wanted the people to stop praising him as they made their way to Jerusalem. The Pharisees recognized Jesus' authority. Any good teacher can make loyal students do their bidding. Make them stop! It is too risky! The Roman soldiers will take note. They are watching who is in the crowd. They're watching you, Jesus! King said, "In the end, we will remember not the words of our enemies, but rather the silence of our friends." If human beings are silent, God will enliven inanimate things to speak. Martin Luther King, Jr. did not want a rock to cry out for him. He believed that God's justice would eventually prevail and he wanted to be found on the Lord's side.

For Discussion
Have there been times when you should have spoken up but remained silent?

Life's Most Persistent and Urgent Question

For King, "Life's most persistent and urgent question [was], 'What are you doing for others?'" He continued his concern about all poor people by planning the Poor People's Campaign (May-June 1968) that he did not survive to see come to fruition. When Barack Obama ran for president, his overriding concern was that no one should have to suffer through a healthcare system the way his dying mother had. He wanted to do something for others. The Affordable Care Act, also known as "Obamacare," is a first step in helping all Americans, who are required by law to have car insurance if they own a car, to have health insurance, giving an ability to receive appropriate treatment to their diseases. In this way, President Obama, a devout Christian, is being "like Jesus," promoting a ministry of healing for all Americans. King was doing his best to be "like Jesus," trying to bring good news to the poor with a five-point Economic Bill of Rights.

What are we doing for others? How are we trying to be like Jesus? How are we participating in the fulfillment of his mission statement? Will we betray the Gospel by being silent, by being co-opted by our own good fortune? Or will we walk together with the least and the lost, marching up to Zion, showing the world that we love Jesus and his way, and stopping to take praise breaks whenever we see the works of God?

For Discussion
What are practical ways that you are touching lives to help people experience the good news of Jesus Christ?

References
*http://www.commercialappeal.com/news/2010/sep/12/photographer-ernest-withers-fbi-informant/
**http://antiwar.com/orig/bromwich.php?articleid=12844